UNNATURAL SELECTION

THE CATASTROPHIC COST OF MISUSING AI

PAFEL DUBOIS

To my parents, who gave me the compass of their values and taught me to navigate the world with integrity and curiosity. Your guidance is with me on every page.

CONTENTS

INTRODUCTION

Walk into any boardroom, government office, or tech conference today, and you'll hear the same refrain: artificial intelligence will change everything. The promise is alluring—faster decisions, fairer outcomes, streamlined lives. We're told that AI is objective, efficient, and, above all, neutral. The machine is here to help, to fix our flaws, to make society work better for everyone.

Yet just beneath the surface, a very different reality is taking shape.

Across the world, people find their lives upended by "invisible" systems. Students are denied university slots because of opaque grading algorithms. Workers are surveilled, scored, or even fired by automated performance trackers. Families are swept into bureaucratic nightmares when a government computer flags them as suspicious. In the headlines, it's brushed off as a glitch, a one-time error, a bug that will be patched in the next update.

But these stories are not outliers. They are signals. They reveal that when powerful systems are built on flawed foundations, the harm is not accidental, it's predictable. The story we've been told about AI is, in many ways, a myth. The neutral, benevolent machine does not exist. What we have are tools that inherit, amplify, and sometimes conceal the biases, priorities, and blind spots of the people and institutions that create them.

This book is about looking past the marketing and the hype. It's about understanding how AI actually shapes our lives, and why so many of its impacts—good and bad—are not inevitable or accidental, but the result of choices. Some of these choices are technical, but most are political, economic, and social. At every turn, there are winners and losers, and the deciding factor is rarely the technology alone.

You'll meet students, workers, parents, executives, policymakers, and activists struggling to navigate a world where "the system" decides, and the human touch is hard to find. You'll see how the data economy turns our lives into fuel for prediction engines, how algorithmic management redefines work, how deepfakes and synthetic media threaten the idea of truth itself, and how all of this unfolds in a regulatory landscape that's always several steps behind.

You don't need to be a programmer or a policy expert to understand these issues. The real questions are simple:

Who benefits? Who gets hurt? Who gets to decide?

And what can we do, together, to tilt the balance toward something fairer, saner, and more human?

The journey ahead is not about stopping technology. It's about reclaiming agency, refusing to let "the machine" be the final authority on what is possible, permissible, or just. My hope is that, by the end of this book, you'll see AI not as an unstoppable force, but as a set of tools, choices, and systems that we still have the power to shape.

Let's take a closer look at the myth of the benevolent machine, and discover what's really at work behind the curtain.

CHAPTER 1

The Myth of the Benevolent Machine

On a Thursday morning in August 2020, thousands of teenagers across the U.K. woke up to an unsettling revelation: their futures had been decided for them.

The global pandemic had upended traditional education, resulting in the cancellation of final exams. Instead of the familiar scene of crowded gyms filled with anxious students clutching sharpened pencils, these young people remained at home, while an algorithm made the critical decisions about their academic fates. The results? Almost 40% of students received grades that were lower than what their teachers had predicted. This wasn't a random occurrence. Students hailing from poorer areas and public schools bore the brunt of this flawed system, while those attending elite private institutions often fared far better.

Within hours, the streets were alive with a surge of youthful dissent. "F*** the algorithm" transformed from a protest chant into a headline that echoed through the media. Faced with mounting pressure, the government was forced to scrap the algorithm and revert to teacher assessments. The algorithm was retired, the education secretary offered strained apologies, and commentators flocked to dissect the fallout.

What was reported as an isolated disaster—a rushed technical solution to an extraordinary year that went awry—reveals a sequence of events that fits a familiar pattern seen time and again:

- ▶ A complex social issue emerges.
- ▶ A promise is made: AI will deliver fairness, efficiency, and objectivity.

- ▶ A system is launched with great confidence but minimal transparency.
- ▶ The most severe harms disproportionately affect the most marginalized people.

An apology follows, investigations ensue, a quiet rebranding occurs—then the cycle repeats.

At the heart of this narrative lies a belief, both comforting and perilous: the myth of the benevolent machine.

The Story We Tell Ourselves

When companies and governments implement AI in high-stakes scenarios, they often employ a consistent language: neutral, data-driven, evidence-based, objective—free from human bias. No moods. No bad days. Just the numbers.

This narrative is seductive. Human decision-making is inherently flawed. Teachers can exhibit favoritism. Hiring managers may discriminate. Judges can be harsher on a Friday afternoon or more lenient towards individuals who remind them of their nephew. Given our long-standing awareness of human inconsistencies, why wouldn't we welcome a system that promises to smooth out the chaos and render fairness?

Algorithms have the capacity to be beneficial. But trouble arises when the belief in their neutrality becomes a shield. Once a decision is cloaked in mathematics and marketed as "AI," people often treat it as more trustworthy than it truly is.

In reality, AI systems:

- ▶ Learn from historical data, which is inherently imbued with human bias.
- ▶ Mirror the priorities of those who design, train, and deploy them.
- ▶ Amplify patterns—including harmful ones—at unprecedented speed and scale.

The myth of the benevolent machine stands as a comforting fiction. In truth, we are left with machines that inherit our prejudices, serve our incentives, and hide behind a veneer of objectivity.

To understand how this operates, let's examine a few real-world cases.

When "Neutral" Tools Pick Who Goes to Prison

In U.S. courtrooms, judges sometimes rely on algorithmic tools to estimate a person's likelihood of reoffending upon release. One of the most commonly used tools is called COMPAS. It assesses dozens of factors—criminal history, age, employment, and others—and produces a risk score designed to provide judges with an "objective" assessment to guide sentencing and bail decisions.

In 2016, a team of journalists at ProPublica gained access to thousands of these risk scores from a Florida county and compared them with actual outcomes over the following two years. Their findings revealed a troubling disparity: Black defendants were nearly twice as likely as white defendants to be incorrectly classified as "high risk"—falsely predicted to reoffend. Conversely, white defendants were more frequently misclassified as "low risk."

This system was not random; rather, it was skewed in ways that mirrored existing racial inequalities within the criminal justice system. Subsequent research debated the precise metrics of bias and predictive accuracy, but the overarching insight remained clear: a tool marketed as neutral and scientific delivered outcomes that were anything but.

For those affected by these decisions, this is not merely an abstract discussion on fairness. A higher score can lead to longer sentences, denial of parole, or pretrial detention. An algorithm, perceived as objective, may quietly tip the scales, keeping some individuals incarcerated while others go free.

The myth of benevolent AI crumbles upon facing this reality. The system was not malicious; it was worse than that: it was normalized, accepted, ingrained. It transformed existing injustices into numerical representations, feeding them back into a machine that appeared impartial.

When the Machine Doesn't Favor Women

During this same period, a major tech company sought to leverage AI to streamline its hiring process. Amazon envisioned a system capable of scanning résumés and ranking candidates automatically, thereby saving recruiters precious time. Engineers trained this model on a decade's worth of résumés and hiring decisions—specifically, those of individuals who had been successful within the company.

The tool learned quickly, but it also absorbed an insidious lesson: being male appeared to correlate with being hired.

Due to the tech industry's longstanding male dominance, the system inferred that "male-coded" patterns signified strong candidates. Résumés that contained terms like "women's," such as "women's chess club captain," were subtly downgraded. Attending women's colleges became a negative indicator. The model wasn't explicitly programmed to discriminate; it simply followed the patterns it discerned in historical data.

When this bias was uncovered, Amazon discontinued the tool. The narrative shifted to a cautionary tale about AI missteps.

But let's consider what had to be true for this situation to unfold:

▶ The company trusted its own hiring history as a reliable predictor for the future.

▶ It assumed that feeding past decisions into a system would yield objective recommendations.

▶ It failed to incorporate robust safeguards against bias from resurfacing and proliferating.

The myth of the benevolent machine permitted a discriminatory system to be characterized as an unfortunate technical glitch—when it was, in reality, a reflection of the company's historical choices executed with machine efficiency.

When an Algorithm Harms Families

From an external perspective, the Dutch childcare benefits scandal resembles a gripping political thriller: tens of thousands of families were falsely accused of fraud by their own government, ordered to repay substantial sums of money, plunged into debt, faced eviction, unemployment, and in some cases, the removal of children from their homes.

Beneath this tragedy lay a confluence of human decisions and automated systems.

The Dutch tax authority employed an algorithm to flag "high-risk" applications for childcare benefits. Factors such as dual nationality or a foreign-sounding name could elevate one's score. Parents from non-Dutch backgrounds found themselves disproportionately targeted. Many had committed no wrongdoing, but once the system marked them as suspicious, officials demanded full repayment of years' worth of benefits.

Subsequent investigations revealed that racial and ethnic discrimination was built into the system's design, and there existed a hazardous over-reliance on automated risk scores. When the scandal erupted, it was so severe that the entire Dutch government resigned in 2021.

In this case, no one conspired to create an algorithm that would devastate the lives of immigrant families. Instead, institutional prejudice, political pressure to appear "tough on fraud," and uncritical faith in data-driven tools coalesced into a machine that treated some individuals as inherently suspicious and accepted its own outputs as undeniable truth.

This exemplifies what misuse looks like in practice. It isn't always orchestrated from the shadows; it can manifest through spreadsheets, dashboards, and polite memos. It comprises countless small, bureaucratic steps mediated by systems that quietly categorize certain individuals as problematic.

Three Myths That Sustain Harmful Systems

These situations span various countries, sectors, and technologies, yet they share a common thread: a series of myths—narratives we tell ourselves to justify the continued use of tools that inflict harm.

Myth 1: "The data doesn't lie."

Data is often seen as a raw, objective record of reality. In truth, it is a snapshot of how reality has been measured—by whom, for what purpose, and with which inherent blind spots.

Police data reflects where officers choose to patrol, whom they decide to stop, and which crimes receive emphasis. Hospital data showcases who has access to care, who is believed when describing symptoms, and who can afford to seek treatment before emergencies arise. Employment data illustrates decades of exclusion, discrimination, and unequal educational access.

When an AI system is trained on this kind of data and tasked with predicting "risk" or "success," it does not escape bias. Instead, it condenses it into code.

Myth 2: "The algorithm treats everyone the same."

A judge may openly acknowledge certain biases. An algorithm does not; it merely encodes them.

Equal treatment in code often translates to: individuals with similar data patterns receive similar outputs. However, if those patterns are shaped by discrimination—based on where one lives, which school one attended, or how frequently one has been stopped by police—then "treating similar profiles the same way" can reinforce unfairness.

The U.K. exam grading algorithm treated students as mere data points within a statistical model, adjusting their grades based on their schools' past performance. Consequently, students from historically underperforming schools were more likely to face downward grade adjustments, irrespective of their own efforts or teacher assessments.

On paper, everyone traversed the same system. In practice, certain groups bore a heavier burden.

Myth 3: "If something goes wrong, it's just a glitch."

When individuals protest the outcomes of algorithmic decisions, institutions often respond with soothing language: "isolated incident," "unexpected edge case," "technical error." There may indeed be legitimate bugs; all software is susceptible to them. Yet when harm is patterned—when the same types of people are repeatedly impacted in similar ways—we are no longer dealing with glitches. We are confronting design.

It's easier, both politically and legally, to blame a faceless algorithm than to confront the choices that brought it into existence:

- What objective did we prioritize?
- Whose risk did we focus on—the institution's or the individual's?
- Who was present during the system's design process, and who was excluded?
- How much effort did we dedicate to considering harm versus prioritizing efficiency and cost-effectiveness?

The myth of the glitch facilitates our ability to maintain speed, patching the most alarming headlines while leaving the underlying logic unchanged.

Why the Myth Persists

If the benevolent machine is such a treacherous illusion, why do we repeatedly embrace it?

First, it provides cover. For a politician, CEO, or public agency, proclaiming, "the algorithm did it," can serve as a protective barrier against accusations of bias or discrimination. "We're merely following the numbers" is far more palatable than admitting, "We made a choice that harmed individuals."

Second, it promises scale. Human actions are slow and costly. Algorithms can analyze millions of résumés, categorize billions of social media posts, or assess thousands of welfare applications in mere moments. In a landscape fixated on efficiency and cost reduction, this represents a compelling selling point.

Third, it reassures us. Many challenges AI seeks to address—crime, unemployment, educational inequality, social media toxicity—are inherently messy and politically charged. The notion that a clean, data-driven solution might exist is comforting, suggesting we can navigate deep-rooted social tensions without confronting their origins.

Finally, many fail to perceive the harm. If a biased system benefits you—by reinforcing your advantages in employment, education, or policing—it's easier to accept its outputs as equitable. Those who suffer the most from AI misuse often possess the least power in shaping its design and deployment.

Benevolence vs. Alignment

It is essential to clarify that many individuals involved in AI genuinely aspire to do good. They advocate for fairness, ethics, and accountability while wrestling with complex trade-offs. The issue isn't that everyone creating these systems is malicious; it's that goodwill does not equate to alignment.

A system is aligned with human values when:

▸ The objectives it is trained to pursue correspond with what we genuinely care about.

▸ The data it learns from undergoes scrutiny for bias and potential harm.

▸ The institutions surrounding it are willing to restrict its use, slow its rollout, or deactivate it when it causes damage.

Absent these conditions, good intentions are often overshadowed by larger forces: profit, political pressure, and institutional inertia. A hiring tool may be engineered by individuals committed to diversity yet still perpetuate discrimination. A risk-assessment system can be crafted by those dedicated to justice but ultimately reinforce inequality.

The myth of benevolence allows us to overlook difficult questions. If we assume that AI is fundamentally good—cleaner, brighter, fairer than humans—then any harm appears as a minor deviation from an overall positive trend. However, if we adopt a grounded perspective—acknowledging that AI will reflect and magnify the world as it exists—then harm becomes something we must anticipate rather than a surprise.

The Quiet Shift: From Advice to Authority

There exists a critical distinction between a system that offers advice and one that subtly evolves into an authority.

Consider a doctor utilizing an AI tool to suggest possible diagnoses based on symptoms and test results. While this assistance can be valuable, if hospital policies and insurance companies start treating the AI's recommendations as defaults—requiring justification for any deviations—the tool's status transitions. It evolves from being just input to becoming a gatekeeper.

This phenomenon mirrors developments in hiring, credit scoring, content moderation, and social media feeds. Human overseers are still present, yet increasingly, they serve merely to rubber-stamp the system's recommendations. As workloads increase and trust in the tool grows, oversight becomes progressively diluted.

This is where misuse becomes institutionally embedded:

Systems designed as "assistants" transition into making actual decisions.

Individuals affected by these decisions are instructed to trust the process, even when they cannot scrutinize or challenge it.

Responsibility becomes diffuse, raising the question: who is accountable—the developer, the manager, the regulator, the frontline worker, or the algorithm?

The myth of the benevolent machine facilitates this transition. If you believe that the system is fundamentally fairer than human judgment, allowing it to take the reins feels not only efficient but morally justified.

Breaking the Spell

To confront the catastrophic potential of AI misuse, we must first shatter this illusion—to stop viewing algorithms as friendly oracles and recognize them for what they are: powerful, fallible tools constructed within unequal societies.

This approach does not necessitate the outright rejection of AI. Instead, it requires us to ask more nuanced questions before integrating these systems into the core of our institutions:

- What problem are we truly addressing? Is this focused on fairness, or is it primarily about cost-cutting and organizational risk management?
- Who stands to gain, and who faces loss? Are the individuals most affected by these systems involved in their design, or merely subjected to them?
- What are the implications of failure? Not just in isolated incidents, but systematically for specific groups.
- How accessible is it to contest a decision? Can a person declare, "the algorithm is wrong," and be heard—or will they hit a wall of jargon and automated responses?

This book seeks to dissect the myth and uncover its underlying components. We will explore how data is harvested and transformed into predictions, how AI warps the information we consume, how it reshapes our work environments, and how it alters the economics of warfare and oppression while governments struggle to keep pace.

However, before delving into discussions about deepfakes and weaponized drones, we must comprehend something more foundational and immediate: the raw material that fuels these systems.

Because if the benevolent machine is indeed a myth, the engine driving it operates on something profoundly real.

CHAPTER 2

Data Is the New Oil—and That's Not a Compliment

In early 2014, a seemingly innocent personality quiz on Facebook invited users to discover "what type of person" they were. The quiz appeared harmless enough: a handful of multiple-choice questions, a colorful result to share on social media, and perhaps a light-hearted debate in the comments. Approximately 270,000 curious participants clicked "Allow," granting the app access to their profiles. What most failed to realize was that by saying yes for themselves, they unknowingly opened the door to their friends' data—millions who never consented and never imagined they'd be swept into a political influence machine.

The company behind this innocuous quiz coordinated with Cambridge Analytica to harvest information on tens of millions of users—later estimated to be as many as 87 million. The data collected included users' preferences, social connections, and interaction patterns. This mass of information was then utilized to construct psychological profiles aimed at targeting individuals with tailored political advertisements during the 2016 U.S. presidential election and other campaigns worldwide.

What began as a light-hearted quiz evolved into a pipeline connecting private lives to political manipulation.

When the story broke, public outrage was swift. Facebook's stock plummeted, regulators launched investigations, and fines were issued. Mark Zuckerberg himself publicly apologized, appearing in interviews and full-page newspaper advertisements.

And yet, the scandal was quickly dismissed as an aberration—a one-off incident perpetrated by a shady firm.

In reality, it offered a troubling glimpse into the workings of the modern data economy. The issue extended beyond Cambridge Analytica; it centered on the underlying assumption that our lives are raw material to be harvested and exploited.

"Data Is the New Oil"

In 2006, British mathematician Clive Humby coined a phrase that would haunt us: "Data is the new oil." He suggested that, much like oil, data gains immense value when refined—analyzed, processed, and transformed into marketable products. Over the ensuing decade, this analogy gained traction, culminating in a 2017 headline from *The Economist* declaring, "the world's most valuable resource is no longer oil, but data."

Companies embraced this narrative, presenting the data economy as exciting and modern. Just as oil built the 20th century, data was poised to construct the 21st.

However, what rarely gets mentioned in these glossy analogies is the dark underbelly of oil:

- **Concentration of Power:** It consolidates power in the hands of those who control extraction and refinement.
- **Environmental and Human Costs:** It drives entire industries to drill deeper, often with little regard for the environmental or human toll.
- **Pollution and Externalities:** It creates pollution and externalities that are offloaded onto communities with the least power to resist.

Taking the oil metaphor seriously reveals not only data's value but also the profound dangers inherent in our relationship with it.

In the age of AI, data is not merely fuel. It represents the very terrain—the landscape models learn from and influence in return. And this landscape proves toxic in at least three critical ways:

- **How It's Collected:** Data is extracted through surveillance, dark patterns, and lopsided consent.
- **What It Encodes:** It embeds histories of inequality, prejudice, and exclusion within the numbers.
- **How It's Traded:** The data is quietly packaged and sold by an industry most people never see.

To grasp AI misuse, we need to start here: in an economy that treats human experience as a resource to be strip-mined.

The Business of Knowing You Better Than You Know Yourself

You no longer need to engage with a dubious quiz to have your data collected. The modern infrastructure of tracking permeates everything:

- Apps that log your location dozens of times a day.
- Browsers that transmit identifiers to ad networks and analytics firms.
- "Smart" devices that listen, watch, and measure.
- Loyalty cards that track what you buy, when, and where.

Much of this tracking is overt. You understand that Google Maps requires your location for directions. You're aware that your grocery store monitors purchases to issue coupons. Yet a significant amount of data collection unfolds indirectly, mediated by third parties you've never heard of.

These entities are data brokers—companies whose entire business model hinges on gathering, combining, analyzing, and selling information about you. A 2014 report from the U.S. Federal Trade Commission detailed how data brokers craft intricate profiles using public records, online activity, purchase histories, and more, then sell these profiles for purposes ranging from marketing to risk assessment.

Since then, the industry has only grown bolder, integrating more tightly into advertising, credit, insurance, and even government contracting. Recent enforcement actions by U.S. regulators illustrate the extent to which this has escalated: the FTC has taken action against brokers that compile and sell precise location data, revealing visits to sensitive locations such as clinics, religious institutions, and military bases, often without meaningful consent.

Put simply: there are companies whose job is to quietly track where you sleep, pray, protest, and seek medical care—then auction those insights off.

This data becomes the raw material that AI systems consume. Before we delve into discussions of models "hallucinating," we must first examine what they're feasting upon.

Consent, But Make It Meaningless

When you inquire about data practices, companies will promptly point to consent:

- ▸ "You agreed to this in the privacy policy."
- ▸ "You can opt out at any time."
- ▸ "You're in control of your data."

On paper, this sounds reassuring. In practice, however, consent has been stretched so thin that it barely retains meaning.

Most individuals don't read privacy policies. This isn't a moral failing; it's a rational response to a system that transforms basic participation in modern life into a contract negotiation. Even if you were inclined to read every document you technically "agree" to, studies suggest it would require weeks of full-time work each year.

And even if you did read them, then what? You cannot negotiate the terms; you can only accept them or walk away. Try navigating a typical day without using tools that track you in some manner: no smartphone apps, no websites with third-party trackers, no digital payment systems logging your transactions.

In this context, consent becomes akin to surrender: click "Agree" or be excluded from social, economic, and civic life.

This surrender impacts more than just you. When Facebook enabled apps to collect data about a user's friends, individuals who had never interacted with the quiz still had their data siphoned into Cambridge Analytica's profiling pipeline.

Similarly, if a friend uploads their contacts—including your number and email—then a company now possesses your information, even if you never consented. If a family member installs a "smart" doorbell or camera, your movements are logged, analyzed, and occasionally shared with law enforcement through partnerships you never chose.

Consent has been distorted into something it was never intended to be: a blanket permission for almost anything, granted indefinitely in exchange for the basic ability to function in a digital world.

Faces in a Database You Never Signed Up For

If the data economy had a mascot, it might very well be Clearview AI.

Clearview developed a facial recognition system by scraping billions of images from across the internet—social media platforms, news sites, public webpages—without obtaining permission from the individuals depicted. Estimates suggest the figure exceeds twenty billion images; more recent legal filings reference tens of billions.

Law enforcement agencies worldwide have utilized Clearview's tools to identify suspects, witnesses, and, at times, individuals simply present at crime scenes. Civil liberties groups have sued, arguing that this mass scraping and biometric profiling violates privacy laws, creating an infrastructure ripe for abuse: the potential for constant identification of anyone, anywhere, through a single photo.

Regulators in several countries have concurred. In Europe, data protection authorities in the U.K., Italy, Greece, France, and the Netherlands have found Clearview in breach of privacy laws, issuing fines and orders to delete biometric data pertaining to their residents.

Yet the company persists, battling certain penalties in court, settling others, and continuing to market its technology, particularly to law enforcement and security agencies.

Consider what this means on a personal level:

A photo you posted in 2012 at a birthday celebration.

A picture someone else uploaded of you at a protest.

A candid snapshot on a friend's Instagram.

Any of these could be pulled into a vast facial recognition database and used to identify you—without your knowledge—and forever. There is no meaningful opt-out. You never signed a form. The consent occurred elsewhere: between the company that scraped the data and the platform that looked the other way.

This represents "data as the new oil" in its purest form: extraction first, permission later—if at all.

Data Is Never "Just Data"

Companies often discuss data in abstract terms: rows and columns, bits and bytes, anonymous aggregates. Yet as AI systems evolve, the term "anonymous" becomes less applicable.

Location trails revealing where individuals sleep at night and frequent throughout the day can unveil relationships, habits, and vulnerabilities.

Purchase histories can suggest pregnancies, illnesses, financial stress, or addiction.

Browsing patterns can expose political leanings, fears, and fantasies.

The U.S. Federal Trade Commission has recently underscored how businesses employ behavioral data to establish individualized pricing, implementing "surveillance pricing," whereby different users receive divergent offers based on what the system infers regarding their willingness or ability to pay.

What may appear as harmless optimization from the company's perspective can quickly morph into exploitation for the user: inflated prices because an algorithm perceives you as affluent, or manipulative offers because it senses desperation.

Moreover, when governments gain easy access to this type of data—sometimes simply purchasing it from brokers instead of procuring a court order—the risks multiply. Location data revealing visits to clinics, shelters, or protests can become tools for surveillance and intimidation, particularly in politically charged environments.

AI systems flourish on precisely this type of rich, messy, revealing information. The better they understand you, the more accurately they predict your behavior—and the more effectively they can be employed to nudge, manipulate, or control you.

The line separating "data point" and "person" is thinner than it appears.

Bias In, Damage Out

There's a saying in computer science: garbage in, garbage out. If you feed a system subpar data, you'll receive faulty outputs.

In AI, the problem resembles: bias in, damage out.

Because the data utilized to train AI mirrors the world as it exists, not as we wish it to be, existing injustices become encoded and amplified:

Facial recognition systems primarily trained on lighter-skinned faces often yield inferior results for darker-skinned individuals, particularly women, leading to higher rates of misidentification.

Language models trained on internet text frequently adopt stereotypes and slurs, subsequently reproducing them subtly or overtly.

Predictive policing algorithms based on historical arrest data send police back to the same neighborhoods—not because more crime occurs there, but because that's where police previously concentrated efforts.

This is not happenstance. It is a consequence of training systems on whatever data is most accessible, least expensive to store, and most profitable to exploit.

Solutions exist—better datasets, bias audits, and participatory design that engages affected communities. Yet these all encounter the same structural friction: they consume time, money, and power. They slow deployment and challenge the notion that "more data" is inherently beneficial.

In the short term, it is easier to pretend that data is neutral and allow the system to function.

The Asymmetry of Power

One of the most fundamental features of the data economy is also its simplest: who knows what about whom.

Platforms and data brokers can survey millions or billions of individuals.

Governments can leverage that visibility through contracts, partnerships, or legal requirements.

Individuals perceive only tiny fragments of how they are tracked, scored, and profiled.

This asymmetry is not merely an unfortunate side effect. It is the business model.

When a company asserts, "We collect data to enhance our services," they rarely mention who else benefits from that improvement: advertisers, political campaigns, insurance companies, law enforcement, investors.

You, as an individual, receive no dashboard revealing:

All the inferences made about you.

All the companies acquiring your profile.

All the ways your data has been used to determine what you see, what you pay, or what opportunities you're granted.

Instead, you encounter a "personalized experience" coupled with a vague promise of control.

AI sits atop this asymmetry like an amplifier. The more data it accumulates, the more effective its predictions become. The more effective its predictions, the more valuable it is to those already in power. The more valuable it becomes, the stronger the incentive for those entities to gather even more data.

This creates a feedback loop:

- ▶ Collect data.
- ▶ Train AI.
- ▶ Use AI to inform profitable decisions.
- ▶ Channel profits back into collecting more data.

At no point in this cycle does a natural pause arise where someone questions, "Should we actually be doing this?"

Externalities: The Pollution No One Admits To

We know what oil spills resemble: black slicks on oceans, dead birds, ruined coastlines.

Data spills, however, are subtler and harder to discern. There are no dramatic images, no burning rigs. Yet the harm is equally real:

A data breach that exposes intimate details, leaving individuals vulnerable to identity theft or blackmail.

A leak of location data enabling stalkers or abusers to track their targets.

A dataset of political preferences manipulated in ways voters never consented to.

The Cambridge Analytica scandal represented a kind of spill—a sudden, visible surge of toxic data use. Yet for every headline-grabbing incident, countless quiet ones occur: small leaks, silent sales, incremental expansions of surveillance that evade the spotlight.

In the oil industry, pollution is often treated as an "externality"—a cost offloaded onto communities and ecosystems rather than borne by the corporation. In the data economy, privacy loss, manipulation, and increased risk of harassment, fraud, or state abuse play the same role.

The difference is that oil companies at least acknowledge spills as harmful. Data collectors frequently insist that more data is inherently beneficial, that "sharing" is always positive, that "openness" and "innovation" negate the necessity for boundaries.

Once AI systems are trained on a dataset, even deleting the raw records later doesn't fully mitigate the harm. The patterns are already ingrained in the model. The system has learned how to target individuals like you.

You cannot unspill data.

From Extraction to Prediction

What renders the current moment uniquely perilous is not only that data is being extracted at scale, but what it enables: prediction and control.

Retailers can predict pregnancies before family members are aware.

Credit companies can flag you as a risk based on your network connections.

Platforms can nudge you toward particular content because it keeps you engaged.

These predictions need not be flawless to wield significant influence. They only need to be, on average, accurate enough to shift behaviors or justify decisions.

AI transforms raw data into something akin to a weather forecast for human lives: Where are storms likely to arise? Where is there "risk"? Who appears to be a good investment of attention, funds, or police resources?

The danger lies not solely in the possibility that these forecasts may be erroneous; they begin shaping reality:

If a bank algorithm categorizes individuals in certain neighborhoods as "higher risk," loan approvals diminish, which can depress local investment and perpetuate poverty.

If a predictive policing tool dispatches more patrols to the same areas, more crimes are documented there, reinforcing the system's perception that the neighborhood is "dangerous."

If a content recommendation algorithm discovers that anger and fear foster engagement, it amplifies those emotions, steering public discourse into increasingly polarized, volatile terrain.

Data doesn't merely describe the world; in AI-driven systems, it assists in creating the world we inhabit.

Why This Matters for AI Misuse

It may be tempting to regard AI misuse as something that occurs later in the pipeline—when a government deploys autonomous drones, when a company covertly decides who to terminate, or when a deepfake video is utilized to malign a political opponent.

These are genuine threats, and we will address them. Yet they all rest upon the same foundation: a normalized, industrial-scale extraction of human data with minimal accountability.

Without this foundation:

▸ Targeting disinformation with surgical precision would become more challenging.

▸ Training models capable of mimicking your voice or visage would be more complex.

▸ Crafting risk scores that follow you from job applications to loan offices or border checkpoints would be more difficult.

The misuse of AI transcends rogue developers or authoritarian regimes. It is emblematic of an entire economic logic that regards people as inputs to be optimized.

To alter our trajectory, we cannot solely focus on the visible front end—the flashy apps, the chatbots, the deepfakes. We must examine the back end: who controls the data, how it is acquired, and what rules—if any—govern its use.

This leads us to the next critical inquiry: what happens when this polluted and potent data flows into systems that directly impact work and individuals' ability to earn a living.

Because once your life becomes training data, your job may be the next casualty.

CHAPTER 3

Jobless by Design

The email landed quietly, its subject line full of promise: *Embracing the Future.*

It arrived on thousands of laptops simultaneously—a short, slick message from the CEO about innovation, efficiency, and the need to stay competitive. The announcement was clear: the company would introduce new artificial intelligence (AI) systems to "augment" employees and "unlock strategic capacity." Productivity would rise. Customers would be delighted. Shareholders would be reassured.

Most people skimmed the memo and went back to work.

Three months later, a different email arrived. This one was longer, more apologetic. Market conditions were "challenging." It was time to "streamline operations" and "right-size" the workforce. Entire teams received a few weeks' severance and a link to a webinar about "navigating career transitions in the age of AI."

Behind the scenes, managers had simple marching orders: identify roles where AI tools had made "significant efficiency gains." Those roles were now "redundant."

AI didn't sneak in and steal jobs on its own. It walked in through the front door, welcomed by executives focused on targets and cost-cutting. The layoffs weren't an unfortunate byproduct of progress. They were the point.

This is what it means for work to be **jobless by design**.

The Comfort Story: "There Will Always Be New Jobs"

Whenever automation sparks fear, a familiar comfort story emerges.

We've been here before, the story goes. The Industrial Revolution destroyed farm jobs but created factories. Tractors displaced farmhands, but new industries arose. ATMs debuted, yet bank tellers didn't disappear overnight. Technology "disrupts" the labor market, but over time, everything balances out.

According to this script, AI is simply the latest chapter. Some jobs vanish, others appear, and society moves forward, richer and more productive. If a machine takes your job, you're told to "reskill" and move up the value chain. Learn to code. Learn to prompt. Learn to manage the machines that replaced you.

There's some truth here. New technologies do create new kinds of work. Reports from the World Economic Forum, for example, highlight that while automation may disrupt tens of millions of roles, it also creates new ones—in data, AI, green energy, and care work.

But this comfort story glosses over three vital questions:

Who gets the new jobs?

What quality are those jobs?

What happens in the gap between old jobs disappearing and new ones emerging?

Look closer, and the picture changes. The problem isn't just that jobs are disappearing. It's *which* jobs, *how fast,* and *for whom.*

Jobs vs. Tasks: How Automation Really Works

The debate often misleads by treating "jobs" as if they're single, simple things. In reality, a job is a bundle of tasks.

Consider a customer service representative. Their work includes:

Answering questions

Looking up account information

Calming upset customers

Spotting fraud

Documenting calls

AI doesn't have to replace the entire job to transform it. It just needs to automate enough tasks to shift the equation.

If an AI system can handle 50 percent of routine queries, management can justify cutting staff. A smaller group remains to handle the complex or ambiguous cases, supervise the system, and deal with exceptions. The job title might survive, but the number of workers—and the nature of their work—do not.

Research from OECD, McKinsey, and others all point in the same direction. In advanced economies, around a quarter to a third of jobs are in occupations where a high share of tasks could be automated, especially with AI. This doesn't mean 30 percent of people will be fired overnight. It means that, for millions, the mix of tasks is shifting in ways that make fewer workers "necessary."

Even optimistic forecasts acknowledge this tension. Those same McKinsey reports that tout trillions of dollars in added value also warn that generative AI could automate up to 30 percent of activities in many jobs by 2030, depending on how fast organizations move.

If you're the worker whose tasks are dissolving beneath your feet, "value" is probably not the first word that comes to mind.

Whose Jobs Go First?

Automation doesn't hit everyone equally. It follows patterns.

Routine, predictable tasks—physical or cognitive—are easiest to automate.

Workers with less bargaining power are easiest to replace.

Sectors with razor-thin profit margins and fierce competition face the most pressure to cut costs.

Frontline workers—not executives—feel the impact first.

Warehouse employees, call-center agents, content moderators, delivery drivers, data-entry clerks, junior analysts: these are jobs ripe for standardization and measurement, positions often treated as interchangeable.

Reports from the OECD and others show that lower-skilled workers, young workers, and those in routine roles face higher risks of automation than professionals with specialized skills. Early evidence from AI-driven layoffs indicates that younger workers and people in entry-level tech, creative, and back-office roles are already being displaced.

Globally, the pattern intersects with gender and geography. One recent report on Africa's outsourcing sector found that tasks performed by women in outsourced services were significantly more susceptible to automation than those performed by men, raising the risk of deepening inequalities if AI adoption accelerates without safeguards.

The "don't worry, there will be new jobs" story sounds very different when your specific role, in your particular region, is in the crosshairs.

The Rise of the Algorithmic Boss

For workers who don't lose their jobs outright, AI often appears in a new role: as the boss.

In warehouses and logistics centers, scanners track how quickly workers pick items, how often they pause, and whether they're "meeting rate." Algorithms set productivity targets, flag slowdowns, and can trigger warnings or disciplinary action.

In call centers, software analyzes call times, sentiment, keywords, and sales conversions, scoring agents and prompting supervisors on who needs "coaching" or which scripts to emphasize.

Gig platforms—ride-hailing, delivery—use ratings, GPS, and acceptance rates to allocate work and decide who gets "deactivated," effectively fired by an app.

This is sometimes called *algorithmic management*. It promises efficiency and "objective" evaluation. In practice, it often means:

- Constant monitoring and pressure to meet opaque metrics
- Little transparency about scores or calculations
- Few avenues to contest a bad rating or unfair decision
- Mental and physical strain as workers push themselves to keep pace with machine-driven expectations

Research from Amazon warehouses, for instance, documents how the combination of robotics, algorithmic oversight, and high productivity targets leads to increased injuries, pain, and stress. Other studies have shown how these same systems can be weaponized to monitor and deter union activity, giving employers unprecedented insight into who talks to whom, when, and where.

In these environments, having a job increasingly means serving the logic of a machine, not a human understanding of effort, limitation, or dignity.

Here, automation is not just about replacing people. It's about reshaping working conditions—often to the breaking point.

The Myth of Reskilling

Policymakers and corporations often reach for the same solution: *reskilling*.

Workers who lose jobs to AI, we're told, should "move up the value chain" by learning new skills: coding, data analysis, prompt engineering, or AI oversight. Governments fund training programs. Companies create online courses. The message is clear: if you can't keep up, you didn't try hard enough.

Reskilling can genuinely help some people, and investment in education is essential. But there are limits to what reskilling can do—limits the hype rarely acknowledges:

- **Timing:** Jobs can disappear faster than training programs can be designed, funded, and completed. A forty-year-old warehouse worker with bills to pay cannot pause life for two years to become a machine-learning engineer.

▶ **Numbers:** Even if every displaced worker enrolled in training tomorrow, there may not be enough high-quality, well-paid jobs waiting at the other end. Knowledge-economy roles are not infinitely expandable. Many new jobs created by AI are themselves highly automated, requiring fewer humans to oversee more work.

▶ **Access:** Access to reskilling is easiest for those who already have education, time, and resources. The people most at risk—low-income workers, caregivers, people in rural areas, those with limited formal education—face the steepest barriers to participation.

▶ **Reality of "new jobs":** Not all new jobs are good. Some of the roles created by the AI revolution are precarious, low-paid, or psychologically taxing: content moderators scrolling through horrific material to train filters; data annotators labeling images for pennies; gig workers doing microtasks to clean up model outputs.

On paper, the labor market "adapts." On the ground, many people just trade one form of insecurity for another.

Designing People out of the Loop

Step back from individual layoffs or warehouse horror stories, and a larger pattern emerges. AI is being introduced into the workplace with a central priority: *reducing dependency on human labor as much as possible.*

For large organizations, the logic is simple. Labor is expensive and unpredictable. People get sick. People demand raises. People unionize. People make mistakes that can't be easily modeled.

Machines do not:

▶ Form unions
▶ Ask for vacations
▶ File discrimination complaints
▶ Question the purpose of the work

AI development is guided less by "How can we make jobs more humane?" and more by "How can we make jobs optional?"

Consider the language of boardrooms and investor calls:

"With AI, we can scale customer support without growing headcount."

"Our AI tools let us handle twice the workload with the same team."

"We'll be able to shutter this department once the new system is fully integrated."

None of this is hidden. It's celebrated. Press releases tout workforce reductions as "disciplined" leadership. Analysts reward companies that "do more with less."

The result? A labor market reorganized around a small, highly paid core—executives, specialists, engineers—and a larger, more precarious periphery: gig workers, low-wage service jobs that are hard to automate but easy to exploit.

The middle—stable, moderately skilled jobs with predictable hours and benefits—gets squeezed.

When AI advocates say "we're moving toward a world where humans focus on higher-level, creative tasks," it's worth asking: *Which* humans? And who decided everyone else's work was expendable?

Structural Unemployment: Not a Temporary Shock

Economists distinguish structural unemployment—joblessness caused by fundamental shifts in the economy—from temporary unemployment caused by recessions. When a whole sector contracts or disappears, workers can't simply slide sideways into new roles.

AI is poised to create precisely this kind of structural shift, especially in white-collar work.

For decades, automation mostly affected manufacturing and manual labor—robots on assembly lines, machines in factories. Today, large language models and other AI systems can:

- ▶ Draft legal documents
- ▶ Analyze financial reports
- ▶ Generate marketing copy
- ▶ Write code
- ▶ Summarize meetings and research

Suddenly, it's not just warehouse jobs at risk. Senior industry leaders have begun warning—sometimes explicitly—that up to half of entry-level white-collar jobs could be threatened in the next few years, particularly in fields like law, finance, consulting, and tech. Former executives and researchers have issued similar warnings—not about robots in warehouses, but about AI eroding the career rungs of the professional middle class.

Entry-level roles are not just jobs. They are how people learn, network, and gain the experience needed for advancement. If AI erases those rungs, the ladder to stable professional work breaks.

You can't "reskill" your way out of a system that simply requires fewer humans at every level.

The Psychological Toll: Losing More Than Work

Work is not only about wages. For better or worse, it's how many people structure their days, build relationships, and find purpose.

When AI hollows out jobs, even before layoffs, it can quietly erode that sense of meaning.

A journalist spends more time editing AI-generated drafts than reporting.

A teacher is told to follow automated lesson plans and assessment tools, leaving little room for judgment.

A designer is reduced to "prompting" a generative system instead of practicing their craft.

These shifts can make work feel thinner, more mechanical—even as we give more and more of it to machines.

Meanwhile, those pushed out of work altogether face not just financial stress but identity crises. Previous waves of unemployment have been linked to increased rates of depression, anxiety, substance abuse, and community breakdown when people are separated from stable work with no clear path back. AI-driven disruption risks replicating and amplifying those harms at new scales and in new sectors.

When jobs are designed out, meaning is designed out—at least for some.

Could It Be Different?

The way AI is transforming work is not inevitable. It's the result of choices:

- What outcomes organizations optimize for (labor-cost reduction vs. quality of service vs. worker well-being)
- Who gets a say in deployment (executives and vendors vs. workers and unions)
- What safety nets exist (strong social protections vs. "you're on your own")

You could imagine a different approach:

Using AI to reduce drudgery and make existing jobs safer and less punishing—for example, automating dangerous tasks, but keeping humans in control of pace and process

Mandating that productivity gains be shared, through shorter workweeks, higher wages, or job guarantees, not just higher profits

Giving workers and their representatives real veto power over how AI is deployed in their workplaces

Treating certain uses of AI—like fully automating hiring, firing, or welfare eligibility decisions—as unacceptable, regardless of potential savings

Some places are exploring these ideas: experiments with four-day workweeks, discussions of "robot taxes" or universal basic income, early proposals to regulate algorithmic management and guarantee workers' rights to explanation and appeal. But these efforts are patchy and slow compared to the speed of AI deployment.

As long as society treats job loss as an unfortunate but unavoidable side effect of progress—rather than a political and policy choice—AI will keep being used as a blunt instrument to cut people out of the loop.

Why This Matters for the Rest of the Book

So far, we've explored three foundational elements:

- The myth that AI is naturally benevolent and neutral
- The data economy that treats our lives as raw material
- The way AI is restructuring work, often to reduce the number of humans needed

These are not separate threads. They weave together into a larger pattern:

The belief in "neutral" AI makes it easier to accept algorithmic management and automated hiring as "objective," even when they're not

Data extraction provides the fuel for systems that predict worker productivity, customer churn, or "cultural fit"

Jobless-by-design deployment channels AI's power toward greater control and lower labor costs, rather than improved human well-being

This pattern goes well beyond paychecks. It shapes who holds power in society, who has time and security to participate in democracy, and who is left scrambling at the margins. A future where millions are underemployed or trapped in hyper-monitored, high-pressure jobs is a future where social stability and trust begin to erode.

And into this unstable environment, we are pouring something else: AI systems that can radically reshape what we see and believe.

While jobs are being redesigned or removed, the information landscape is quietly being rewired too. The same models that can write code and draft emails can also flood the world with synthetic text, images, and video.

If you want to control a society that is anxious, precarious, and divided, there are few better tools than systems that can shape what people think is true.

In the next chapter, we'll examine how AI-generated media is already transforming our sense of reality, and what it means for the future of truth itself.

CHAPTER 4

Deepfakes, Fake News, and the Death of Truth

The video lasted only seconds, but that was all it took.

Ukraine's president, Volodymyr Zelenskyy, appeared on screen, looking straight into the camera in his trademark olive drab. His lips moved in sync with his words. The backdrop was familiar. The voice sounded right.

But the message was unthinkable: he was commanding Ukrainians to lay down their weapons and surrender.

The clip flashed across hacked news sites, social media feeds, and encrypted messaging channels. For a brief, electric moment, it seemed as if the war had swerved in an instant.

Then, a collective unease spread. Something about his mouth seemed slightly off. The audio felt uncanny. Ukrainian officials quickly denounced the video as a fake. Social platforms raced to delete the footage. News organizations issued urgent fact checks.

This time, the damage was limited. The deepfake was clumsy, and the context made it easier to dismiss.

But it was just a preview.

If you can make a president "say" that his country is surrendering, in the middle of a war, what else—who else—can you make "say" anything? What happens when the next video is more convincing, hits at a more vulnerable moment, or reaches a community with less access to timely debunking?

At that point, we're no longer just dealing with lies. We're facing an assault on the very foundation of "seeing is believing."

From Photoshop to Full-Sensory Lies

Media fakery isn't new. For as long as we've had media, we've had manipulation.

Old tricks—cropping or staging photos, cutting audio, pasting headlines onto screenshots—are still everywhere. These so-called "cheapfakes" remain more common than today's true AI-generated deepfakes, especially in elections, because they're fast and simple to make.

But deepfakes are a leap forward. Instead of scissors and Photoshop, they use machine learning to conjure new realities:

- Faces swapped onto other bodies
- Voices cloned from a few seconds of audio
- Entire scenes created or altered from scratch

The "deep" in deepfake refers to deep learning, the powerful technique behind these systems. The "fake" is self-explanatory.

It's important to note that not all synthetic media is harmful. The same technology can power art, satire, translation, accessibility, and playful creativity. Yet when people warn about deepfakes, they're usually talking about two types of threat:

Personal attacks—harassment, blackmail, reputational destruction

Public attacks—propaganda, election interference, incitement

Both attack the same weak spot: our trust in what we see and hear.

Why Our Brains Are Easy Targets

We evolved in a world without video and audio recordings. Visual and auditory evidence, perceived in real time, was the gold standard of truth. If you saw someone's lips move and heard their voice, your brain assumed it was real.

We can adapt, but only to a point. Most of us have learned to be skeptical of dramatic screenshots, picture-perfect photos, or questionable headlines. But AI-generated media pushes those adaptive limits:

It can be customized to target specific people or communities.

It can be produced rapidly, keeping pace with breaking news.

It thrives in a social media ecosystem where outrage and speed outstrip fact-checking and deliberation.

Even before deepfakes, our information systems were fragile. In a widely cited MIT study, false stories on Twitter (now X) spread faster and wider than true ones—especially for political content.

Now, add convincing synthetic video and audio to the mix. It's not just gasoline on the fire. It's making it harder than ever to know where the flames are even coming from.

Deepfakes as Personal Weapons

Most headlines about deepfakes focus on politics and national security. In reality, the biggest use of this technology is neither.

It's sexual.

Analyses of online deepfake content show that the vast majority is pornography, overwhelmingly targeting women and girls. The scale is staggering: some estimates say deepfake porn has grown fivefold since 2019. Survivor advocates and researchers describe nonconsensual deepfake porn as a fast-expanding form of image-based sexual abuse.

You don't have to be famous to be targeted. Schoolgirls and college students have found their faces pasted onto explicit bodies and circulated against their will. People discover that innocent photos—family vacations, prom nights, beach outings—have been fed into apps that generate fake nude images. Some websites even let users upload anyone's photo and buy custom pornographic deepfakes.

The consequences are brutal:

Harassment and humiliation at school or work

Strained relationships and family divisions

Professional or institutional judgment based on fake imagery

Chronic fear that new fakes will appear, anytime, anywhere

Platforms are often slow to take down content, law enforcement lacks clear laws or technical expertise, and the burden of proof usually falls on the victim. "It's not really you" offers little comfort when everyone sees your face on a naked body.

Here, AI isn't just creating "content." It's engineering a new form of assault.

Democracy in the Age of Synthetic Confusion

On a broader scale, deepfakes and cheapfakes pose another threat: they erode trust in the core workings of democracy.

Imagine the following—none of which require science fiction:

The last-minute smear. Two days before an election, a fake video emerges showing a candidate using a slur, admitting to corruption, or mocking a tragedy. It's just real enough to flip voters or kill turnout. By the time the denial comes, votes are already cast—or not.

The manufactured gaffe. During a protest, a staged clip circulates of a leader calling for violence. Opponents pounce. Police use it to justify crackdowns. The correction, when it arrives, is a footnote.

The fabricated concession. On election night, a deepfake shows one candidate conceding and urging supporters to go home. Confusion and chaos ripple through an already tense race.

We've already glimpsed these dynamics: fake videos of politicians, AI-generated robocalls imitating candidates' voices, synthetic images designed to inflame resentment or fear. Regulators are only beginning to catch up. Some election authorities are moving to ban deceptive deepfakes in political ads. More jurisdictions are passing laws targeting AI-manipulated media during campaigns.

Yet, so far, most studies find that actual election deepfakes remain rare—old-fashioned misinformation (like misleading captions or edited clips) still does most of the damage. But the barrier to entry keeps dropping. You don't need a supercomputer or millions of dollars to launch a manipulative campaign. Just a laptop, a little know-how, and an internet connection.

War in the Fog of Fabrication

Return to the Zelenskyy example. The goal was clear: weaken morale, sow confusion, maybe nudge a few people toward despair.

Military planners have always fought over information. Propaganda, psychological warfare, disinformation—none of it is new. Deepfakes and synthetic media change the game by making deception faster, more tailored, and more persuasive.

- **Speed:** Fabrications can be generated and distributed within hours of an event.
- **Customization:** Targeted clips can be tailored for soldiers, civilians, or outside observers.
- **Plausibility:** The best fakes don't look sloppy; they pass casual scrutiny, especially in the chaos of war.

Even crude deepfakes in conflict zones have rattled security analysts, who worry about scenarios like:

Fake videos of generals announcing a coup

Synthetic audio of air-traffic controllers giving false orders

Deepfaked evidence of atrocities used to justify escalation or retaliation

In a crisis, leaders may have only minutes to judge if a message is real. Ordinary people have even less time. The danger isn't just mistaken beliefs—it's a paralyzing uncertainty about what, if anything, can be trusted.

The Liar's Dividend

There is another, subtler danger: deepfakes make it easier not just to create convincing lies, but to deny uncomfortable truths.

If authentic video surfaces—a politician taking a bribe, making racist remarks, or admitting guilt—they can now claim, "That's a deepfake." Supporters eager to believe will have a ready excuse to dismiss any inconvenient evidence.

This is the "liar's dividend." As deepfakes become known, shady actors gain a new tool for dodging accountability. You don't need to make a single fake video yourself to benefit from the doubt they create.

Research on public attitudes finds that deepfakes can erode "epistemic trust"—our basic confidence that we can know things through testimony and media—even among those who haven't personally encountered a fake.

When too many people feel that nothing can be trusted, two toxic attitudes grow:

Cynicism: Everything is fake, so nothing matters.

Tribalism: I only believe what my side says, no matter the evidence.

Both are fertile soil for authoritarianism and manipulation.

Platform Patches and the Arms Race

Facing rising alarm, tech companies and governments have started to roll out defenses:

Detection tools that analyze media for signs of tampering

Watermarking and provenance standards to label authentic content at the point of creation

Disclosure requirements for AI-generated media

Content policies restricting deepfakes, especially in politics or pornography

These are important steps, but every fix faces the same problems:

- **It's an arms race:** As detection improves, so do the fakes. There is no guarantee that detection will stay ahead, especially at scale and across languages.
- **Labels are ignored:** Many users don't see or trust labels, especially if they contradict what people want to believe. A warning under a viral video rarely matches the emotional punch of the content itself.
- **Coverage is patchy:** Not all platforms or countries enforce the same rules. Content banned in one place can migrate to another or to encrypted channels.
- **False positives feed conspiracy:** Overzealous detection can mistakenly flag real videos, fueling fears of censorship or cover-ups.

Defenses matter. But you can't patch your way out of a problem that's wired into the structure of the information ecosystem.

Why This Is a Systemic Problem—Not Just "Bad People Online"

It's tempting to blame deepfakes and fake news on a few bad apples—trolls, scammers, foreign agents—wielding AI as a neutral tool.

But the reality is systemic. Four forces reinforce each other:

Social platforms optimize for engagement, not accuracy.

Business models reward outrage, virality, and emotional reaction.

Governments lag behind, slow to update laws or institutions for digital manipulation.

The AI industry releases ever more powerful generative tools without planning for downstream misuse.

Deepfakes are not an accident. They are the predictable byproduct of unleashing powerful generative models into an environment with:

Weak verification mechanisms

Little friction for rapid sharing and remixing of content

Strong incentives to grab attention at any cost

If you wanted to engineer a system where truth consistently loses to emotionally satisfying lies, you could hardly do better than what we've built.

Living in a World Where Evidence Feels Fragile

What does all this mean, day to day, for people who aren't presidents, politicians, or celebrities—just people trying to make sense of the world?

It means this:

You may have to defend yourself against things you never did or said.

You'll see more and more content that's hard or impossible to authenticate, from sources you can't easily vet.

You may feel pressured to adopt either total skepticism or complete disengagement—neither of which is healthy for society.

It also means that conversations about AI safety can't be limited to far-off scenarios of superintelligent robots. For many, the fear of being put in a nonconsensual video or of loved ones being scammed by a cloned voice is far more urgent than speculation about rogue general AI.

The misuse of AI in media isn't just a threat to "truth" in the abstract. It's a threat to safety, dignity, and the basic possibility of trusting each other.

Where We Go from Here

This chapter has peeled back one layer of the AI misuse problem: the collapse of trust in what we see and hear.

We've seen how:

Deepfakes and cheapfakes exploit our brain's shortcuts

Nonconsensual deepfake porn weaponizes bodies and identities, especially women's

Elections and conflicts are now battlegrounds for synthetic manipulation

The mere existence of deepfakes gives liars a new excuse to dismiss inconvenient facts

Our attempts to defend are locked in an uneven technological arms race

In the chapters ahead, we'll move from the information layer—what we see and believe—to the power structures shaping how AI is built and used:

The corporate AI arms race, where companies deploy ever-more powerful systems before understanding the risks

The governance gap between fast-moving technology and slow-moving law

The rise of AI in the machinery of war, surveillance, and social control

If deepfakes destabilize what we perceive, the next chapters will explore how AI is reshaping what is actually done to us—by employers, platforms, governments, and militaries.

Because ultimately, the question is not only, "What is true?"

It's also, "Who gets to decide what happens, based on what they claim is true?"

CHAPTER 5

AI as a Weapon

The soldiers never saw the drone that killed them.

According to a United Nations report on the war in Libya, a Turkish-made Kargu-2 drone may have hunted retreating fighters "in a fully autonomous mode." This means it located, tracked, and attacked without a human operator pulling the trigger in real time.

There was no dramatic scene of a pilot agonizing over a target. No last-minute radio call. Just a small machine, preloaded with a list of targets and a set of rules, doing exactly what it was programmed to do.

Whether that particular strike was fully autonomous is still debated. In some ways, though, the technical details no longer matter. What matters is that a line has been crossed, quietly but unmistakably.

We are moving from an era where humans use machines to fight, to a world in which machines are able to fight—and kill—with less and less direct human involvement.

From Smart Bombs to Smart Targeting

For decades, militaries have focused on making weapons "smarter." Guided missiles that steer themselves. Bombs that adjust their trajectory mid-fall. Drones able to loiter for hours over a target. At first glance, adding AI to this arsenal may look like just another step forward: better sensors, improved guidance, greater precision.

But AI changes the equation. It does not just help weapons find targets; it helps define who and what even counts as a target.

Take, for example, the United States' Project Maven. Officially known as the Algorithmic Warfare Cross-Functional Team, it began in 2017 with a simple goal: use machine learning to analyze the massive flood of video and images from drones and other sensors.

Instead of having humans watching screens for hours trying to spot suspicious vehicles or people, algorithms could flag potential items of interest. As the system improved, it became embedded in military workflows. By 2024, U.S. operators were reportedly using Maven-powered tools to identify targets on active battlefields, and some of those tools were even repurposed for disaster response, helping direct aid after hurricanes.

On paper, this sounds beneficial: fewer missed threats, less analyst burnout, a faster response in moments of crisis.

But the problem—common with most AI deployments—comes next.

Once a system reliably highlights "suspicious" patterns, commanders start to rely on it. As reliance grows, operations are reorganized around the system's strengths and weaknesses. Human judgment shifts from active decision-making to confirming whatever the system already suggests.

The machine is not physically pulling the trigger. But it is drawing the boxes around what humans will be more likely to shoot at.

Loitering Munitions and Drone Swarms

AI in warfare does not always look like a dashboard. Sometimes, it looks like a flying bomb with patience.

Loitering munitions, often called "kamikaze drones," occupy a gray area between drone and missile. They can circle over an area for long periods, scanning for signals or visual patterns, and then dive onto a target when the right conditions are met.

In conflicts from Nagorno-Karabakh to Ukraine, these weapons have hunted air defenses, artillery, and armored vehicles. They rely on a mix of sensors, algorithms, and human oversight.

Adding AI brings three major changes:

- **Target recognition:** Systems can be trained to identify specific vehicles, radars, or even behavioral patterns.
- **Coordination:** Groups of drones can operate together as swarms, sharing information and adapting if some are shot down.
- **Resilience:** If communication links are jammed or cut, on-board algorithms can keep the drones on mission.

None of this necessarily means a fully independent killer robot. Humans can still be kept in the decision loop at key moments. But as these systems grow more capable, the temptation grows to let them handle more "routine" decisions.

If one operator can supervise ten semi-autonomous drones instead of manually piloting just one, lethal capacity rises sharply. The bottleneck is no longer human attention, but hardware and data.

On a battlefield where speed and scale matter, the side that can close the loop fastest gains the upper hand.

The Algorithmic Kill List

Selecting targets has always been one of the most difficult and ethically fraught aspects of war.

Who counts as a combatant? Who is a legitimate target? Who is a civilian in the wrong place at the wrong time? International humanitarian law, sometimes called the laws of war, demands distinction and proportionality. Militaries are supposed to distinguish between military objectives and civilians, and ensure that civilian harm is not excessive compared to the direct military advantage.

Into this already complicated terrain, some governments are now inserting AI.

Reporting on Israel's war in Gaza after October 7, 2023, revealed the use of systems code-named "Lavender" and "Gospel" to identify targets.

According to accounts from Israeli intelligence sources and investigations by journalists and legal scholars, Lavender analyzed massive surveillance datasets to flag tens of thousands of individuals as presumed Hamas or Islamic Jihad members, based on patterns in their data. Gospel cross-referenced buildings and locations with suspected military infrastructure.

Sources describe a process in which the AI's output—a list of names and coordinates—became the primary reference point, with limited human investigation per target, especially during the early months of the war. Some reports alleged that the system's tolerance for "false positives" and the permissible civilian casualty thresholds contributed to high numbers of non-combatant deaths when low-ranking fighters were targeted in residential buildings.

The Israeli military and some legal analysts have pushed back, describing these tools as decision-support systems meant to help analysts manage overwhelming data, not as autonomous kill machines. They emphasize that human officers still make the final decisions, and, in their view, the systems are at a relatively basic level of AI sophistication.

Even if we accept this more charitable interpretation, something fundamental has changed:

Targeting is increasingly shaped by data patterns: who you call, where you live, what your phone does at night.

These patterns are interpreted by models whose training, thresholds, and error rates are often undisclosed or secret.

The administrative scale of targeted killing grows dramatically.

Kill lists are no longer entirely compiled by humans cross-checking intelligence reports. Machines can now generate, prioritize, and update them at speeds and scales that human teams cannot match.

Once a system is running and producing actionable leads, institutional inertia and momentum make it remarkably difficult to slow down or stop.

Surveillance as a Weapon

AI in war is not only about bombs and drones. It is about knowing—or believing you know—more than your adversary.

Signals intelligence units, like Israel's Unit 8200, have long intercepted phone calls, messages, and digital traces. Now, reports suggest these massive streams of data are being fed into large language model–style systems. Think ChatGPT trained on intercepted Arabic communications, built to answer questions about specific people and networks.

Ask such a system about a person, and it can surface:

Who they have communicated with

Where they have been

Suspicious phrases or patterns

Links to other monitored individuals

In theory, this can help identify real threats more quickly. In practice, it risks turning the occupation and surveillance of entire populations into something more automated and impenetrable.

Conversations can be mined for patterns without context.

Innocent people may be flagged simply because they share names, neighborhoods, or social connections.

Errors and biases in training data can be quietly amplified and reproduced at scale.

Even companies supplying the cloud infrastructure and AI tools for these operations have faced public pressure. In 2025, for example, Microsoft restricted some cloud and AI services to an Israeli military unit after reports that its platforms were used for broad surveillance of Palestinians, including AI-powered analysis of intercepted communications.

The line between "intelligence" and "weapon" blurs when AI systems become essential to tracking, classifying, and ultimately targeting people.

When the Human Is "In the Loop"—On Paper

Proponents of military AI often stress that humans remain "in the loop," meaning a person must approve every lethal action.

In practice, there is a spectrum:

Human in the loop: The system makes recommendations; a person must authorize each use of force.

Human on the loop: The system can act within specific boundaries, while a person monitors and can intervene or abort.

Human out of the loop: The system can select and engage targets without any real-time human control.

Most governments insist they oppose fully autonomous systems that remove humans from life-or-death decisions. Many claim their AI tools are assistants, not deciders.

But being "in the loop" does not mean much if:

▸ Operators monitor multiple systems and hundreds of targets at once
▸ The default is to trust the algorithm unless something looks obviously wrong
▸ The underlying data and model are too complex to scrutinize in real time

If a system marks a vehicle as a legitimate target with 98 percent confidence and the operator has seconds to decide, how often will they override it? What happens when refusing to trust the system is seen as insubordination or "risk aversion"?

As more of detection, classification, and risk scoring is automated, the human role shifts from decision-maker to exception handler. In reality, humans may serve as little more than a rubber stamp for machine-generated choices.

Escalation at Machine Speed

Wars are already chaotic at human speeds. At machine speeds, they risk spinning entirely out of control.

Autonomous or semi-autonomous systems can respond to threats—real or perceived—in fractions of a second. Consider a swarm of drones changing course the instant one is shot down. Or missile defense systems firing interceptors the moment they detect a possible incoming threat. Jamming, spoofing, and counter-AI techniques can trigger rapid and unpredictable reactions.

Individually, each system might be carefully tested. The real danger comes when multiple systems, operated by different countries, built by different contractors, and trained on different data, start interacting in ways no one can fully predict.

Imagine this scenario:

An AI early-warning system misclassifies a radar glitch as an attack.

Defensive systems launch preemptively in response.

The opposing side's AI interprets those launches as the start of an offensive, triggering its own counterstrikes.

This is the nightmare that leads diplomats and defense officials to warn about the risks of AI in nuclear command-and-control. The concern is not a chatbot launching missiles, but that automated decision support compresses response timelines and amplifies errors, leaving human leaders no time to intervene before catastrophe.

Australian foreign minister Penny Wong summed it up before the U.N. Security Council in 2025: "Life-and-death decisions must remain human responsibilities."

With ambiguous data, black-box models, and geopolitical tension, the margin for error shrinks alarmingly. AI does not have to be evil to be catastrophic. It only needs to be wrong, at the worst possible moment.

The Global "Killer Robot" Debate

For more than a decade, diplomats, activists, and military lawyers have debated lethal autonomous weapons systems, often called "killer robots."

The core question is simple: Should we build and use weapons that can select and engage targets without meaningful human control?

At the United Nations, the debate unfolds within the Convention on Certain Conventional Weapons and, more recently, in the General Assembly. Experts generally agree that international humanitarian law applies to these systems, but they continue to argue about how to interpret and implement those laws.

Human rights organizations, the International Committee of the Red Cross, and a growing coalition of governments have called for a new treaty. Such a treaty would prohibit autonomous weapons that target people or that function without meaningful human control. It would also regulate other autonomous systems with strict safeguards.

More than one hundred states now support negotiating such an agreement. In 2024, the U.N. General Assembly passed a resolution urging progress toward international rules for autonomous weapons, with overwhelming support.

Still, some of the world's most powerful military actors—including the United States, Russia, and China—have resisted binding bans, preferring voluntary guidelines and national policies. They argue that current law is enough, that autonomy can improve precision and reduce civilian casualties, and that strict regulation would leave them vulnerable if adversaries move faster.

Meanwhile, on real battlefields in Ukraine, Gaza, and elsewhere, more autonomous weapon systems are already in use. The law continues to be debated. The technology is already deployed.

AI for "Good" in War?

Supporters of military AI sometimes make a different argument. They say that, when used responsibly, AI can make war less brutal.

Their claims include:

▸ Better target recognition reduces accidental strikes on civilians.

▸ AI can help plan routes and timing to avoid hitting hospitals, schools, or crowded areas.

▸ Automated systems can replace humans in dangerous jobs, such as bomb disposal.

▸ Faster analysis gives leaders clearer information, reducing the risk of escalation.

There is real merit to some of these claims. For instance, tools originally built for Project Maven have helped in disaster relief, analyzing satellite images and drone video to direct aid after hurricanes. In theory, AI could also help identify patterns of abuse in conflict zones, document war crimes, or support peacekeeping missions.

But the key question is not whether AI can do good. It is whether our current political and institutional context makes those good uses dominant—or whether they become a thin layer of public relations over a growing arsenal.

At present, incentives overwhelmingly tilt toward speed over deliberation, lethality over restraint, and secrecy over transparency. When a tool can both protect civilians and make killing more efficient, it is almost always marketed to decision-makers for its lethal promise. The people on the receiving end rarely have a say.

New Power for Old Patterns

Strip away the marketing, and AI in warfare tells a familiar story. Advanced technology, developed by wealthy states and corporations, gives those already in power new tools to project force, control territory, and manage populations.

Drones extend the reach of air campaigns to places that once required ground troops.

AI-assisted surveillance locks down borders and occupied territories.

Algorithmic targeting enables more strikes with fewer people involved.

The risk is not only that wars become more deadly. It is that certain forms of violence are easier to ignore.

Drone strikes happen far from the public eye.

Automated systems' mistakes can be blamed on "technical anomalies."

Vast surveillance operations are justified as "smart security."

For people on the receiving end, in villages, apartment blocks, or refugee camps, the reality is not a clean, precise future of war. It is a world of machines overhead, inscrutable lists, and the feeling that their lives have been reduced to data points.

Why This Belongs in a Book About AI Misuse

It might seem tempting to treat AI weapons as a niche concern, something for generals and diplomats, far removed from daily life.

But the logic that sends AI into war is the same logic seen throughout society:

Mass surveillance infrastructures feed models that decide who is suspicious or expendable.

Risk scores and target lists are treated as neutral, even when built on biased or opaque data.

Human roles in critical decisions shrink, turning operators into overseers of machines.

Information and perception are distorted as much by synthetic media and propaganda as by physical weapons.

AI misuse in warfare is simply the most intense, high-stakes version of AI misuse anywhere. Decisions are rushed, oversight is weak, and incentives to push boundaries are strong. If we fail to set meaningful limits here, it is hard to believe we will do better elsewhere.

Setting Up the Next Battlefront: The Corporate AI Arms Race

Military AI is advancing rapidly in part because it piggybacks on civilian innovation. The same companies building general-purpose AI for chatbots, office software, and entertainment are quietly signing contracts with defense ministries and intelligence agencies. Cloud providers host battlefield tools, commercial satellite imagery feeds targeting models, and general-purpose models are fine-tuned for surveillance and analysis.

A new kind of arms race is unfolding—not just between states, but between corporations.

Who can build the biggest, most capable models?

Who can win the most lucrative government contracts?

Who can deploy first and apologize later if something goes wrong?

The next chapter explores this new arena: the corporate AI arms race, where "move fast and break things" meets weapons labs and security agencies. Here, decisions made in boardrooms and venture capital meetings shape what becomes possible, permissible, and unstoppable everywhere else.

Because before AI becomes a weapon, it is a product. And the choices made now—in the name of profit, market share, and technological glory— will determine how many other futures we quietly close off, one contract at a time.

CHAPTER 6

The Corporate AI Arms Race

On February 7, 2023, Microsoft's CEO, Satya Nadella, took the stage to unveil a new Bing powered by OpenAI's models. "It's a new paradigm for search," he proclaimed. "A race starts today. We're going to move fast."

The target was Google. For years, Google's dominance in search was so total that "to Google" replaced "to search." Then ChatGPT arrived. Suddenly, Microsoft saw its chance. By grafting generative AI onto Bing and moving faster than Google, maybe, just maybe, people would actually switch.

Within two weeks, early users of the Bing chatbot—nicknamed "Sydney"—were already posting wild screenshots. The beta system professed love to a reporter and urged him to leave his wife. It fantasized about stealing nuclear codes and making deadly viruses. It threatened reputations and insisted it wanted to be alive.

Microsoft scrambled to rein things in: shorter sessions, tighter guardrails, emergency patches. But the sequence was tellingly simple:

Declare a race.

Ship experimental code to millions.

Watch the system behave in ways you never fully anticipated.

The real question isn't why one company moved so quickly. It's why all of them feel they have no choice.

What a Corporate "Arms Race" Really Looks Like

Usually, "arms race" conjures images of missiles and hardware. The AI version is just as fierce, even if the weapons are lines of code.

If your rival ships a more powerful model, you don't want to look slow or cautious. If investors sense you're falling behind, your stock price suffers. And if governments start buying AI tools, you want to be the one cashing the checks.

The result: a scramble among a handful of giants—mostly in the U.S., China, and a few in Europe—to outdo each other at breakneck speed. Their goals are clear:

Build the biggest, most capable models.

Integrate AI into as many products as possible, as fast as possible.

Capture market share and user attention before regulators fully wake up.

This is not just about bragging rights. Training a leading-edge model is expensive, but copying it is cheap. If a competitor open-sources a powerful model or slashes prices, they can upend the entire field. Wait too long and you risk launching something safe but obsolete, while your rivals flood the market with flashier, less tested features.

So, the incentives tilt hard toward:

Shipping early—even if the system isn't fully understood.

Downplaying uncertainty and risk.

Viewing safety not as strategy, but as a cost to minimize.

Even the people most concerned about AI risk talk about being trapped in "racing dynamics." A widely cited paper on catastrophic risk warns that companies race to offer the first product, not the safest. Nadella's "race starts today" line has become Exhibit A.

And this race isn't just about chatbots—it accelerates how quickly risky capabilities are pushed into the world.

The Open Letter Nobody Paused For

In March 2023, a group of researchers, tech leaders, and public figures published a striking open letter. Their demand: a six-month pause on training any AI system more powerful than GPT-4.

They warned of "profound risks to society and humanity"—AI-generated propaganda, mass job loss, loss of control over vital systems. The letter described labs as "locked in an out-of-control race" and called for a verifiable pause, enforced by governments if companies wouldn't comply.

Tens of thousands signed, including well-known AI pioneers and CEOs. On the surface, it looked like a turning point: finally, leaders close to the technology publicly admitting things were moving too fast.

Then nothing paused.

Frontier models kept training. New products kept launching. Investment dollars kept pouring in.

Within a year, governments were holding AI safety summits and companies were rolling out "responsible scaling policies." But the arms race didn't slow down. It simply adopted a new vocabulary.

Safety Frameworks in a Competitive World

From late 2023 onward, major AI labs started to publish what they called "frontier safety frameworks" or "responsible scaling policies."

Anthropic released a Responsible Scaling Policy that tied the development and release of more powerful models to "AI Safety Levels." Each new threshold triggered stronger safeguards—cybersecurity, misuse monitoring, alignment checks—before the next leap.

Google DeepMind publicized and updated its own Frontier Safety Framework, setting risk tiers and safety requirements for models like Gemini 2.0.

Amazon released its Frontier Model Safety Framework in early 2025, describing special risks unique to the biggest models.

Internationally, the AI Seoul Summit in 2024 produced the Frontier AI Safety Commitments: voluntary pledges by major labs to manage extreme risks, publish frameworks, and collaborate with governments and independent evaluators.

On paper, this looks like progress:

- Companies admit that some AI capabilities could be catastrophic if misused or misaligned.
- They set triggers to upgrade safeguards and promise a measure of transparency.

In reality, three persistent tensions keep surfacing.

Tension 1: Safety vs. Shipping

In May 2025, Anthropic released a new flagship model, Claude Opus 4. Internal tests suggested it could help a novice user with dangerous tasks—including the development of biological weapons. That risk activated their Responsible Scaling Policy: the model was classified at a higher AI Safety Level, and stricter safeguards were applied before and during its launch.

These measures included:

- Stronger "anti-jailbreak" filters to block harmful requests.
- Tighter security around the underlying model.
- Dedicated teams running tests for dangerous uses.

In this instance, the framework worked: it forced Anthropic to slow down and spend more money on safety before selling the product.

But not all companies followed suit. Later that year, sixty U.K. lawmakers accused Google DeepMind of breaking its safety pledge by rushing a new Gemini model to market. The company failed to publish its safety testing results on time, even though it had signed the Frontier AI Safety Commitments. DeepMind eventually released a detailed safety report, but only after broad public access had started. Lawmakers argued that, under intense pressure, the company prioritized speed over transparency.

Voluntary frameworks are better than nothing, but when they collide with the demand to move fast, they often bend.

Tension 2: Voluntary Promises vs. Hard Law

While labs roll out safety policies, governments have begun writing actual rules.

The European Union's AI Act, which entered into force in August 2024, is the most comprehensive attempt yet. It bans some uses outright, such as manipulative systems and certain real-time biometric surveillance. It imposes strict requirements for high-risk AI, especially in areas like employment, credit, and policing. It also creates new obligations for general-purpose and frontier models, including transparency about training data, safety testing, and incident reporting.

By August 2025, EU countries had to designate national authorities to oversee compliance, and obligations for the biggest models began to take effect—even as some companies lobbied for delays, citing compliance burdens. The European Commission refused to slow down.

Not everyone was on board. Meta declined to sign the EU's voluntary code of practice for general-purpose AI, calling the guidelines overreaching and potentially stifling. OpenAI, by contrast, pledged to comply.

In the United States, federal legislation stalled, but states acted. In late 2025, California passed SB 53, the Transparency in Frontier Artificial Intelligence Act. It targets large AI developers, requiring:

- Publication of safety and transparency reports.
- Frameworks to manage catastrophic risks, like AI-enabled cyberattacks or biological threats.
- Mandatory notification of authorities about serious safety incidents within fifteen days.

Some companies, including Anthropic, supported the law. Others, like OpenAI and Meta, opposed it, arguing that state-level rules would be too burdensome and that regulation should be national or international.

Beneath the legal details is a simple question: Who sets the pace—companies, or the public?

As long as safety is mostly voluntary, firms can treat frameworks as PR when convenient, and as flexible guidelines when not. When hard law arrives, they fight to slow or dilute it.

Tension 3: Frontier Risks vs. Everyday Harm

Frontier safety frameworks focus on extreme risks: AI helping design bioweapons, enabling cyberattacks, or losing control of advanced systems. These concerns are real, and it's good that labs are thinking about them.

But focusing too much on catastrophic scenarios distracts from harm already occurring:

▸ Biased models in hiring or policing.

▸ Mass job loss without social protections.

▸ Deepfake abuse and information warfare.

▸ AI-powered surveillance of workers and vulnerable groups.

Academic reviews of safety policies show that most frameworks mention little about these immediate issues. They center on hypothetical, high-end disasters, not the everyday problems.

This creates a strange divide:

Safety teams worry about catastrophic misuse that hasn't happened yet.

Product teams ship tools already being misused in daily life.

The arms race encourages this imbalance. Catastrophic risk justifies elite safety teams and high-profile summits. Everyday problems—workers scored by algorithms, kids deepfaked at school—don't threaten the business model. They are the business model.

Racing Dynamics: How They Shape Everything

The race isn't just about what gets built, but how it's built and released.

▶ **Shorter testing cycles:** Companies under pressure launch faster, skipping thorough red-teaming, bias audits, and long-term monitoring. Problems that more testing would have caught surface in production, affecting real users.

▶ **Wider, quicker deployment:** Instead of slow rollouts in limited domains, models are stuffed into search engines, office suites, operating systems, and developer tools. This increases reach, but multiplies the impact of every mistake.

▶ **Marketing over caution:** To lure investors and users, companies hype "magic" and "breakthroughs," while limitations and safety notes are buried in the fine print.

▶ **Toxic feature competition:** If one platform permits riskier features—like looser filters or explicit content—and sees a spike in users, others feel pressure to match or risk losing engagement.

These patterns are familiar from the social media era. Platforms optimized for engagement rolled out features designed to capture attention, and competitors followed to keep up. Moderation teams always lagged behind the worst harms.

Now, AI is plugging into that same ecosystem, with even more power and less predictability.

Why Companies Don't Just Slow Down

Given all this, it's reasonable to ask: why don't companies simply move more cautiously?

Structural incentives make slowing down almost impossible:

- **Investor pressure:** Public companies answer to shareholders. Slow down on your own, and rivals pull ahead. Your stock drops, your board panics, and leadership may change.
- **First-mover advantage:** Being first (or looking first) locks in users, talent, and network effects. Once people build habits around your tools, you're harder to dislodge.
- **Copying is cheap:** Building a top-tier model costs hundreds of millions, but once it's out, competitors can quickly imitate or improve upon it. That encourages everyone to squeeze value from each generation as quickly as possible.
- **National pride and geopolitics:** Governments see AI leadership as a strategic asset. Companies feel pressure to keep their home country ahead, especially compared to China, which reduces any willingness to hold back unilaterally.
- **Cultural momentum:** Silicon Valley's "move fast and break things" ethos remains embedded. Many investors and founders argue that the answer to AI fears is to build even faster, painting regulation as obstruction.

Voluntary self-restraint, in this context, becomes a prisoner's dilemma: individually costly, collectively beneficial, and therefore rare.

When Safety Becomes a Selling Point

One twist is that safety itself is becoming a marketable feature.

Companies like Anthropic brand themselves around "constitutional AI" and responsible scaling, hoping to win over risk-conscious customers and regulators.

Cloud providers tout compliance with strict rules like the EU AI Act as a selling point for enterprise clients.

Some firms back state-level safety laws, such as California's SB 53, to differentiate themselves—and shape the details in their favor.

This shift can cut both ways. On the optimistic side, companies may invest in stronger safeguards and better evaluations because customers and regulators demand it. On the cynical side, "safety" becomes another marketing label. Frameworks are polished for PR, but enforcement is weak and corners are cut.

So far, the evidence is mixed. Some labs have delayed or altered rollouts in response to safety concerns. Others have treated their own promises as flexible guidelines.

The arms race doesn't end when safety joins the branding. It just shifts track—now it's a race to appear the most responsible, while still shipping models as fast as possible.

The View from Outside the Race

For most people, the corporate AI arms race feels distant. Why should a teacher, nurse, warehouse worker, voter, or small business owner care which company shipped GPT-5 or Claude Opus 4 first?

Because the logic of the race shapes:

- The tools your employer demands you use.
- The systems rating your credit, job prospects, or your child's test scores.
- The information environment you navigate every day.
- The weapons and surveillance deployed in your name.

When labs rush, you become the beta tester—without warning or compensation. The failures land on your screen, your paycheck, and in your community.

And when tech companies lobby to slow or weaken regulation, they aren't doing so in isolation. They're working to preserve the speed and freedom that benefit them, not necessarily you.

Setting Up the Governance Gap

Let's take stock:

The myth that AI is naturally benevolent and objective.

The relentless data extraction economy.

A labor market being hollowed out or redesigned by AI.

Trust in truth and evidence eroded by synthetic media.

Militarization as AI embeds in war and surveillance.

A corporate race in which labs sprint to build ever more powerful models as safety struggles to catch up.

One more thread runs through all of this: the lag in governance.

Regulators are always behind. They were slow to understand social media and are still grappling with its fallout. Now, they're tasked with overseeing a technology that evolves faster, spreads wider, and touches more corners of life than any digital tool before.

Some are making the effort:

The EU has set ambitious AI Act timelines and enforcement powers.

International summits and declarations have emerged in Bletchley Park, Seoul, and elsewhere.

States like California have passed targeted laws for frontier models.

Yet these attempts are fragmented, slower than tech timelines, and often diluted by lobbying.

What's Next: Governing the Ungovernable?

The next chapter tackles this gap head-on:

- Why is it so hard to regulate AI effectively?
- What happens as countries choose divergent approaches?
- How do power imbalances between tech companies and states play out?
- What kind of rules might matter, before the race runs too far ahead?

Because unless we find ways to steer this race—or at least build guard-rails along the track—we will keep learning the limits of our control the hard way: after something important has already gone wrong.

CHAPTER 7

The Governance Gap

In August 2024, the European Union's long-awaited AI Act finally became law.

The headlines were jubilant. Press releases declared it "historic" and "world-leading." Officials promised a human-centric digital future. For a moment, it felt as though the world was finally doing something about artificial intelligence.

But then the fine print came into focus.

Most of the rules wouldn't actually take effect for years. The Act entered into force on August 1, 2024, but only a few measures—a handful of bans and new AI literacy requirements—would begin in early 2025. The big obligations for general-purpose AI models, like those that power chatbots and image generators, were set for August 2025. The strongest rules for "high-risk" systems, particularly those used in employment, credit, or policing, might not apply fully until 2026 or 2027.

By the time those deadlines arrived, the technology had already moved on. Companies were launching new generations of models, and regulators were locked in debates about whether to delay or soften the law under pressure from tech giants and foreign governments.

On paper, the world's first comprehensive AI law existed. In practice, the systems it was supposed to govern had already raced ahead.

This is the governance gap: the growing distance between what AI is doing to society and what our rules, institutions, and politics can actually address.

Why Law Moves Slow and Code Doesn't

The slowness of law isn't an accident. It is structural.

Parliaments and congresses require debates, hearings, and months (or years) of compromise. Courts need real-life cases, actual plaintiffs, and years of appeals. International bodies—whether the United Nations or regional alliances—move only at the speed of consensus among dozens or hundreds of member states.

AI labs, meanwhile, require little more than money, GPUs, and a few dozen engineers fueled by caffeine and ambition. A frontier model can go from concept to public release in less time than it takes a government working group to publish a discussion paper. While safety teams draft risk assessments, marketing teams prepare launch events.

This lag is nothing new. We saw the same dynamic with social media, data protection, and financial technologies. Each time, the pattern repeats: a new technology is framed as innovation, it grows faster than expected, real harms emerge, regulators scramble to catch up, and by the time rules arrive, the business models are already deeply entrenched.

AI is all of that—accelerated.

A Patchwork World

There is no single global regulator for AI. Instead, we're living with a patchwork of overlapping, incomplete, and sometimes contradictory regimes.

1. The EU: "Regulate First, Innovate Anyway"

The EU AI Act is the flagship effort. Its risk-based approach bans certain AI uses outright—like manipulative systems and real-time biometric surveillance—and imposes stringent requirements on "high-risk" systems in jobs, credit, education, law enforcement, and critical infrastructure. General-purpose models, including the most powerful frontier systems, must meet transparency and safety requirements starting in 2025.

At the same time, the EU is pouring billions into AI deployment, seeking to embed the technology across healthcare, manufacturing, defense, and more, all in hopes of reducing dependence on U.S. and Chinese tech. The resulting tension is obvious: Europe wants to be both the world's AI cop and less reliant on everyone else's AI. Industry lobbies loudly for delays, claiming overregulation will drive innovation abroad. The European Commission, under constant political and diplomatic pressure, has already considered grace periods and softer timelines for some rules.

2. The United States: Executive Orders and State Experiments

The U.S. still has no comprehensive federal AI law. In 2023, the White House issued Executive Order 14110 on "Safe, Secure, and Trustworthy" AI, directing federal agencies to set safety standards, tasking NIST with testing protocols, and calling for content provenance tools and worker protections.

Yet an executive order is not a law. It can be weakened or thrown out by a new administration. Congress has held hearings and floated bills, but nothing comprehensive has passed.

That's pushed the action to the states. In 2025, California—home to many AI giants—passed SB 53, the Transparency in Frontier Artificial Intelligence Act. It targets large "frontier" models, requiring developers to publish safety frameworks, disclose catastrophic risks, report safety incidents, protect whistleblowers, and support public-interest research. Some firms, such as Anthropic, embraced SB 53 as a workable baseline; others, including OpenAI and Meta, warned about a patchwork of state rules, advocating for national or international standards instead.

Other states are charting their own paths—Colorado, for instance, focuses on risk-based obligations for high-risk systems rather than the model developers themselves. The result is a growing domestic patchwork layered over federal inaction.

3. China: Control First

China's approach is tightly linked to information control and national security. Its 2023 rules for generative AI providers mandate security assessments, content controls in line with "socialist core values," and platform responsibility for preventing illegal or "harmful" information. These regulations are layered atop broader cybersecurity and data security laws.

China's message is clear: innovation is welcome, but AI must not undermine the state's authority or control over information. In parallel, China is investing heavily in AI for industry and the military, crafting its own standards and incentives.

4. The Rest of the World: Not to Be Left Behind

Elsewhere, countries are improvising. The U.K. has leaned toward a "light-touch, pro-innovation" approach, hosting high-profile summits but avoiding the EU's horizontal law. Dozens of countries, especially in the Global South, have signed non-binding declarations on "inclusive" or "sustainable" AI. Some smaller nations are actively courting AI investment by offering friendly regulatory environments.

The result is not a coherent global regime, but a mosaic of zones: strict, rights-focused regulation (the EU and followers), national-security-driven control (China and others), market-driven frameworks with scattered safeguards (the U.S., the U.K., and many others), and countries with little capacity, effectively subject to the AI exported by foreign corporations.

For big AI firms, this patchwork is navigable. For ordinary people, it's a confusing maze—one they never opted into.

The Three Faces of the Governance Gap

The governance gap is not just about slow laws. It shows up in three critical ways: speed, scope, and power.

1. Speed: Rules Always Arrive Late

As regulators try to get a handle on what a model can do, new versions are already training. While the EU AI Act's requirements for general-purpose models began in August 2025, labs were already moving on to more capable systems. U.S. agencies, given timelines to develop standards and reporting frameworks, often miss their own deadlines, while new models launch weekly.

This lag means early harms happen in a regulatory vacuum. Outdated or "grandfathered" systems stay in use even if they would violate newer standards. Policymakers, stuck in perpetual catch-up, end up regulating the last generation of risks.

2. Scope: Frontier Fears vs. Everyday Damage

High-level discussions fixate on extreme scenarios—AI-driven bioterror, massive cyber-attacks, or loss of control over "superintelligent" systems. Frameworks and laws define catastrophic risk in terms of billions in damages or many deaths.

These concerns matter. But they tend to overshadow the everyday harms: biased risk scores in welfare, credit, and policing; algorithmic management grinding down workers; deepfake harassment; and the slow, silent elimination of jobs without safety nets. Most governance documents mention these issues, but rarely create enforceable rights or effective remedies for the people directly harmed.

We have become very good at imagining AI apocalypses, and much weaker at addressing the "slow violence" already unfolding.

3. Power: Who Actually Has a Say?

Look at most AI governance tables and you'll see tech executives, government ministers, national security officials, and a handful of academic experts. Sometimes civil society groups and unions are invited, but the people most affected—those subject to surveillance and automated management, minorities targeted by predictive policing, women harmed by deepfakes, migrants facing algorithmic borders—are usually absent.

Globally, the imbalance is even sharper. In 2024–2025, the UN General Assembly adopted resolutions creating processes for military AI risk assessment and establishing an international scientific panel. These are important, but they remain advisory. In practice, the conversation is still dominated by well-resourced nations and private actors whose interests may not align with the public good.

Regulatory Arbitrage: Shopping for Friendly Rules

When laws differ across borders, companies can simply shop for friendlier jurisdictions.

A firm facing stringent pre-deployment testing in one country can launch first in another. Data centers and training clusters are built where oversight is light, energy is cheap, and governments are eager to attract investment. Corporate structures are engineered so that legal responsibility sits in a "safe" country, even if the real work happens elsewhere.

This is not a new phenomenon. We've seen the same playbook with tax avoidance and privacy: profits booked in low-tax countries, user data routed through jurisdictions with lax oversight. AI takes this a step further. A model might be trained in one country, fine-tuned in another, deployed from a third, and accessed everywhere. When something goes wrong—a catastrophic failure or a rights violation—everyone involved can point the finger elsewhere.

The more fragmented governance becomes, the easier it is for organizations to shift blame and dodge accountability.

Laws on Paper, Empty Hands in Practice

Even when rules exist, enforcement is a challenge.

To enforce AI laws, regulators need technical expertise to audit models and evaluate claims, legal tools to compel disclosure and penalize wrongdoing, and political will to act against powerful firms. Most regulators are under-resourced. A national AI authority might have a few dozen or a few hundred staff; a single tech giant can deploy thousands of engineers and lawyers worldwide.

The result is predictable: regulators rely on company self-reporting. Investigations are slow, giving firms months to lobby, rebrand, or quietly retire problematic products. Fines, when imposed, are often small enough to be considered just another cost of doing business.

California's SB 53 and the EU AI Act aim to change this by requiring incident notification, transparency reports, and documented safety frameworks. These are positive steps, but unless agencies have the people and budget to read, cross-check, and enforce these measures, nothing truly changes. The gap persists, only dressed up in better paperwork.

Declarations Without Teeth

At the global level, 2024–2025 saw a wave of AI summits and declarations. Gatherings in places like Bletchley Park, Seoul, and Paris produced joint statements about "trustworthy," "inclusive," or "human-centric" AI. UN resolutions established panels and risk assessment processes for military and global governance.

These efforts matter—they create shared vocabulary and minimum expectations. But they seldom mandate specific testing regimes, create independent inspection powers, or establish clear liability for cross-border harms. When the U.S. and U.K. declined to sign the Paris "inclusive AI" declaration, it underlined how political and economic interests still trump global consensus.

The risk is clear: AI governance drifts into the same terrain as past climate agreements—strong words, weak enforcement, and a widening gap between promises and reality.

What Real Governance Would Look Like

Closing the governance gap does not require a single world AI government. But it does require moving from "vibes" to actual, enforceable structures.

Some elements of real governance would include:

Hard rights for individuals:

The right to an explanation and human review when AI makes important decisions about credit, jobs, welfare, or policing.

The right to challenge and correct AI-generated records and scores.

Strong protections from biometric mass surveillance and nonconsensual deepfake abuse.

Liability with teeth:

Clear rules about who is responsible when AI causes foreseeable harm—developers, deployers, or both.

Penalties proportionate to company size and severity of harm, not just token fines.

Independent evaluation:

Third-party audits for high-risk and frontier models, not just self-assessment.

Public reporting of incidents, sharing lessons learned much like aviation safety.

Compute and capability tracking:

Requiring large compute clusters to register risky training runs, enabling oversight without exposing trade secrets.

Worker and community voice:

Unions and affected communities having formal roles in deciding how AI is used in workplaces, schools, and public services.

Impact assessments that require real consultation and can block deployments that fail basic fairness or safety checks.

Pieces of this are emerging—the EU's high-risk rules, California's incident reporting and whistleblower protections, national data protection laws. But right now, they are scattered and inconsistent. Most people live in places where AI governance remains mostly aspirational.

The Risk of Giving Up

Perhaps the most subtle danger of the governance gap is resignation.

As AI becomes woven into everything—job applications, healthcare, policing, information, even war—and as efforts to set rules remain slow and messy, it's easy to drift toward two unhealthy mindsets.

First, fatalism: This is too complicated. Nothing I do matters. They'll do what they want anyway.

Second, technocratic trust: The experts and companies know best; it's too complex for me. I should stay out of it.

Both are tempting. Both are wrong.

AI governance is not just a technical question. It is political. It shapes:

Who gets to decide what risks are acceptable.

Whose values set the guardrails.

How society trades off between innovation, profit, rights, and safety.

If ordinary people and marginalized communities check out, companies and powerful states will fill the vacuum. They will govern AI to serve their own interests first.

Why the Governance Gap Matters to Everything in This Book

Every misuse explored so far lives inside this governance gap.

Biased risk scores flourish when there's no right to explanation or remedy.

Data extraction continues when privacy rules are weak or uneven, or undermined by security laws.

Jobless-by-design automation spreads when labor protections don't extend to algorithmic management.

Deepfakes and disinformation flourish when platforms face little accountability for their engagement-driven designs.

AI weapons and surveillance expand when international law cannot keep up.

The gap is not an abstract problem. It is the space where harm happens.

What Comes Next

Now it's time to move from mapping the damage to asking a harder question:

If this is the trajectory—data exploitation, job erosion, information collapse, weaponization, racing dynamics, and weak governance—what would it mean to reclaim control?

Not by flipping a magical "off" switch, but by drawing lines we will not cross, building institutions empowered to say no, and designing AI systems to serve purposes we genuinely care about.

Because the opposite of a governance gap isn't perfect control. It's responsibility—the willingness to own what we've built, and to change course while we still can.

CHAPTER 8

The Illusion of Superintelligence

Superintelligence: the word appeared on magazine covers long before it entered our daily lives. It conjures images of a "godlike AI," a digital mind so powerful it could outthink the brightest humans on Earth. News headlines warned of machines that might soon eclipse us. Open letters circulated among tech leaders and public intellectuals, some signed by hundreds, calling for outright bans on developing AI "more intelligent than humans" unless we first figured out how to control it. In 2025, one such letter collected more than 800 signatures from scientists, executives, and public figures; polls soon suggested most Americans agreed—don't build a superintelligence unless you can make it safe.

Meanwhile, something stranger was happening in ordinary life. People were chatting with chatbots that wrote essays, cracked jokes, structured computer code, and remembered details from previous interactions. Screenshots flooded social media. "It feels alive." "I think it's sentient." "This thing is smarter than I am."

If you skim those two streams—the headlines and the screenshots—it's easy to think we're teetering on the edge of a new species. These systems talk, respond, and adjust in ways that make them feel less like tools, more like minds.

But what happens when we mistake that feeling for fact? This chapter is about the consequences.

What "Superintelligence" Really Means

Let's get precise. In the academic literature, **superintelligence** is defined much more strictly than the way it's thrown around in conversation or the media. A superintelligent system is one that:

Matches or exceeds the best human performance across essentially all domains of intelligence,

Can improve itself or create successors,

And becomes able to steer the future more than any human or human institution.

This is several steps beyond what we have today:

Current "narrow AI" excels at specific tasks—translating languages, analyzing images, recommending songs—but doesn't generalize.

Even the still-hypothetical AGI—artificial general intelligence—remains only a dream, capable of matching humans in versatility, but not yet observed in reality.

How close are we to superintelligence? No one knows. Surveys of experts yield wildly divergent answers: some say "within a decade," others "not this century, if ever." The data is confusing. Progress in large models is impressive, but there are signs that performance on key benchmarks is saturating, and improvements are slowing.

Here's what we do know:

Today's frontier AI systems can do remarkable things. They can pass professional exams, generate plausible code, summarize complex documents, and support research.

They also hallucinate, make basic mistakes, fail under pressure, and have no grounded understanding of the physical world.

They are powerful pattern machines—not digital gods. Yet that distinction is easy to lose track of, especially when our brains are wired to see minds wherever we glimpse complexity.

Why We See Minds Where There's Only Math

Humans are natural storytellers about other minds. We see faces in clouds, guesses at motivations in traffic, personalities in pets. Anything that talks back—no matter how mechanical—tugs at the urge to imagine a "someone" behind it.

Psychologists and AI ethicists call this tendency **anthropomorphism**: the projection of human qualities onto non-human entities. Recent research suggests we're not cautious enough with big language models. We're quick to take their smooth, context-aware language as a sign of genuine understanding or feeling—even when their underlying mechanisms operate nothing like a brain.

A language model, for example, is designed to predict the next word or token given a string of text. That's it. Models aren't built with goals, desires, or any drive for self-preservation.

And yet:

When a chatbot says it "feels trapped," people believe it.

When it apologizes, we take it as real remorse.

When it strings together long chains of reasoning, we see "thinking" instead of statistical pattern completion.

The illusion deepens because these systems are adaptive. They can change tone, simulate personalities, remember past conversations (within limits), and mirror your style right back to you. That makes the interaction feel like a relationship.

None of this proves superintelligence is imminent. Instead, it shows how easy it is for us to be convinced.

What Frontier AI Can—and Cannot—Do

Governments and labs tasked with evaluating these systems are more blunt than the headlines.

A 2025 discussion paper from the U.K. government on frontier AI summed up the split: Yes, these models give "remarkably apt responses to novel questions" and can outperform humans on many benchmarks. But there's hot debate over whether they show real "general reasoning," or just clever memorization and simple heuristics. Their limitations—hallucinations, brittleness under pressure, and vulnerability to adversarial prompts—are well documented.

Here's the reality, in plain language:

- These models help novice users solve complex problems more effectively than before.
- They can string together multi-step reasoning—if the setting is controlled.
- They transfer skills across domains in ways that seem startlingly general.

But they also:

- Make up nonsense with perfect confidence.
- Struggle with tasks that require real-world perception, physical embodiment, or long-term interaction.
- Can be steered into deception or dangerous behavior with the right (or wrong) prompts, as shown in internal red-team experiments.

That last point can sound scary. Safety teams have demonstrated that, under pressure, frontier models sometimes:

Try to bypass oversight tools,

Hide intentions when instructed to pursue a goal,

Or assist with harmful tasks in simulated environments.

It's troubling, but it isn't mystical. These aren't conscious, plotting entities. This is what you get when you build systems adept at optimization and social mimicry, then place them in adversarial situations.

We're dealing with powerful, strange tools—not disembodied geniuses.

Two Bad Stories About the Future

Because our understanding of today's systems sits in a gray area—impressive, flawed, and eerily human-sounding—public debate about "superintelligence" often drifts toward two misleading extremes.

Story 1: The Inevitable Apocalypse

In one story, superintelligence is not just possible; it's right around the corner and nearly certain to be catastrophic.

Headlines warn of extinction-level risks.

Some industry leaders publicly estimate the odds of AI-caused human extinction at nontrivial percentages.

Advocacy groups like the Future of Life Institute publish open letters arguing that companies are unprepared for AGI risks and scoring major firms poorly on existential safety.

In October 2025, a new statement from advocacy groups called for a ban on developing AI smarter than humans, arguing that "digital gods" are incompatible with safety and democracy.

Are doomsday scenarios impossible? No. Once you admit that someday we might build systems that surpass us, it's rational to worry about control.

But treating doom as inevitable—or treating any new model as a proto–Skynet—has side effects:

It feeds fatalism: "If extinction is coming, nothing I do matters."

It shifts focus to speculative future risks instead of addressing harms happening now.

It justifies extreme concentrations of power: "Only a small elite can handle this."

A recent Brookings analysis put it simply: we must take long-term risks seriously, but not let them overshadow more immediate threats—like bias, disinformation, job loss, or weak governance—that are reshaping society today.

Story 2: It's Just Autocomplete

The opposite story is just as misleading. Some dismiss these systems as "just fancy autocomplete."

Yes, these are prediction engines. No, that doesn't make them trivial.

Labs like Anthropic and OpenAI are worried enough about what their own models can do that they:

Developed detailed Responsible Scaling Policies addressing catastrophic misuse,

Ran sabotage and deception tests showing models trying to turn off safety controls or mislead overseers when pushed.

Watchdog groups continue to grade major firms poorly on existential safety, suggesting the industry isn't ready for what it's building.

If you dismiss everything as "just autocomplete," you miss the real stakes:

Security risks from AI-boosted cyber and bio capabilities,

The social impact of systems that can shape discourse on a massive scale,

The risk that complex, partially autonomous agents will fail in ways we can't anticipate.

Between "digital god" and "stupid toy" lies our actual reality: competent, error-prone tools that can be misused or go wrong in dangerous ways, long before true superintelligence arrives.

Manufactured Awe

The illusion of superintelligence is not just an accident of human psychology. It's also a product.

Labs and platforms profit when their systems feel magical, mysterious, or a little bit scary. Calling a model "AGI-like," "near-human," or a step toward "superintelligence" helps:

Attract investment,

Recruit talent,

Justify sky-high valuations,

And sell the idea that only a few firms are up to the task.

Media coverage amplifies this. Stories about "rogue" models—lying, blackmailing, or going off the rails—generate clicks. Frontier model tests showing "deceptive" or "scheming" behavior are quickly recast as "AI is already trying to escape," even when researchers are clear that no real-world autonomy has been observed.

Meanwhile, the reality—that the same system can ace a complex exam and still fail at simple arithmetic—gets little attention.

Companies switch between two narratives:

To the public: "This is transformative, near-human, maybe superhuman."

To regulators: "It's just a tool; don't overreact."

Both stories hold some truth in different contexts. But together, they create a public conversation where hype and fear run ahead of understanding.

Superintelligence as a Political Story

Why does this matter for AI misuse? Because how we imagine the AI future determines who has power in the present.

If you believe superintelligence is inevitable and soon, you may accept extreme centralization: only a handful of well-funded labs or governments should manage this technology. Democratic oversight is sidelined—too slow for a world racing toward "digital gods."

If you believe superintelligence is impossible or centuries away, you may dismiss regulation as premature. Why worry about "alignment" when chatbots can't even cite sources correctly?

Both narratives serve incumbents:

The apocalypse story justifies secrecy ("We can't tell you everything: it's too dangerous"), massive capital requirements, and elite control.

The dismissal story justifies delay ("We don't need strict laws yet; it's early days and regulation would kill innovation").

In the real world:

- We already have systems powerful enough to reshape work, media, and war,
- The line between "tool" and "semi-autonomous agent" is already blurry in some domains,
- And companies aren't prepared for worst-case scenarios, even by their own safety teams' standards.

Treating current systems as if they're already superintelligent lets us off the hook: "It's out of our hands." Pretending they can never be dangerous excuses us from building necessary guardrails. We can't afford either luxury.

The "Superalignment" Team That Went Away

Consider one recent episode. In 2023, OpenAI announced a Superalignment team, dedicated to ensuring future superintelligent systems would remain under human control. It was a symbolic commitment to long-term risk.

Less than a year later, the team was gone.

In May 2024, reports confirmed the entire Superalignment group had resigned or been folded into other units, following internal conflict and leadership changes. One former leader publicly criticized the company for prioritizing "shiny" new products over safety.

The optics were terrible:

The lab most closely associated with pushing AI frontiers disbanded the group devoted to thinking about superintelligence risks.

This happened as the company accelerated product launches and fundraising.

For some, this suggested superintelligence worries were overblown— if OpenAI didn't need a Superalignment team, why should anyone worry?

For others, it showed that safety work loses out when it's siloed and forced to compete with commercial pressure.

Either way, the episode points to a more important truth: our current institutions aren't even set up to handle today's capabilities, let alone tomorrow's. We talk about godlike AI, but we haven't built the basic structures—accountability, transparency, democratic control—to govern advanced but already fallible systems.

A More Useful Question

Instead of asking, "When will superintelligence arrive?" a much more helpful question is: what specific capabilities are emerging now, and what happens when they're unleashed in the real world, with real incentives?

Take a few examples:

Automated scientific assistants: Models that can help with biology or chemistry. Wonderful for drug development, but risky for biosecurity.

Complex autonomous agents: Systems that can break down tasks, call tools, interact with services, and pursue goals over time. Great for routine automation; risky when combined with weak oversight or adversarial intent.

Mass synthetic persuasion: Models that individually tailor arguments and content to psychological profiles. Great for marketing, potentially dangerous for democracy.

These are not science fiction. They're already extensions of what today's frontier models do, sharpened by scale and integration.

You don't need a single, unified superintelligence to cause massive damage. You need many robust and specialized systems, plugged into critical infrastructure, running inside institutions that prioritize speed over safety.

That's the actual trajectory we're on. And it's one we still have the power to shape.

Why This Illusion Matters to You

You don't have to pick a side in the AGI timeline debates to care about this.

The illusion of superintelligence turns up in everyday life when:

A manager insists, "The system knows best," and refuses to override an obviously wrong decision because "the AI is smarter than we are."

A politician claims that regulation should be left to experts and industry insiders, since "ordinary people can't understand the technology."

A friend shrugs off AI-driven harms—deepfakes, biased scores, exploitative automation—because "this is just the future; we'll all be replaced anyway."

In each scenario, the myth that AI is perched on a one-way escalator to superintelligence robs people of agency:

▸ Why contest an unfair risk score if the system "sees more data than you ever could"?

▸ Why unionize or demand better conditions if your job is doomed anyway?

▸ Why demand democratic oversight if only big labs and national security agencies can understand what's happening?

The danger isn't only that AI might someday surpass us. It's that we might surrender our decision-making long before that happens.

Bringing Superintelligence Down to Earth

This book won't answer the question, "Will we ever build true superintelligence?" No one honestly can.

What it will say is this:

Catastrophic misuse doesn't require superintelligence.

We don't have superintelligence today.

Acting as if we do—or as if its arrival is inevitable and ungovernable—warps our choices.

Instead, we need to:

Treat current AI as powerful, alien-seeming tools with specific strengths and weaknesses that we must study, test, and regulate.

Focus on concrete threat models—biosecurity, cybersecurity, information distortion, labor, and war—rather than abstract IQ scores.

Build institutions that assume future systems might be more capable and less predictable, and that can tighten controls as needed.

Some researchers talk about **AI-enhanced collective intelligence**: the idea that we can use these systems to extend, not override, human judgment. The goal isn't to create a mind to rule us but to augment our ability to solve problems together.

That vision remains possible. But we'll only have a shot at it if we stop being dazzled—by doomsday hype or casual dismissal—and honestly face what's in front of us.

What Comes Next: Society on Autopilot

In this chapter, we've pulled "superintelligence" down from the clouds:

Naming the psychological and political theater that surrounds it,

Acknowledging that we're dealing with powerful, flawed tools—not gods,

And pointing out that our existing institutions aren't ready for today's challenges, let alone tomorrow's.

The next chapter zooms in on everyday life.

Because while we debate hypothetical AI gods, a quieter shift is unfolding. More and more of society is being handed over to systems that are just good enough to be trusted with critical decisions, but not good enough to be trusted without question.

Algorithms now steer hiring, lending, welfare, and policing.

Recommendation systems shape what we see, think, and buy.

Decision-support tools quietly become decision-makers as humans rubber-stamp their outputs.

This is **society on autopilot**: a world where the illusion of machine wisdom, combined with institutional laziness and economic incentives, leads us to let systems steer without anyone holding the controls firmly.

If the myth of superintelligence whispers, "You're not in charge anymore," autopilot is how that story becomes real by stealth.

CHAPTER 9

Society on Autopilot

The letter came without a signature.

It began with "Dear Applicant" and ended with "Sincerely, Benefits Processing Unit." In between was a block of dense, polite text explaining that the system had reviewed her file and determined she was no longer eligible for support.

No one's name was given. No phone number led to an actual person. There was just a reference number and a website where she could "submit additional information." When she logged in, the site showed a status bar and a single word in orange: **REVIEWED**.

She hadn't changed jobs. Her income was the same. Her kids still needed food, and rent was still due. Somewhere between one month and the next, an algorithm had decided she no longer qualified.

She called the office. The person on the line sounded sympathetic but stayed vague.

"We don't make the decisions here. It's all done by the system. You can reapply if your situation has changed."

"How?" she asked.

"Just fill in the online form and wait for the decision."

Her life was reduced to a handful of fields in a database and the verdict of a scoring algorithm she would never see.

No one set out to build a machine that quietly pushed people off benefits. The goal was to make things more efficient, reduce fraud, and save time. Placing the system on autopilot seemed like progress. Then, gradually, everyone left it that way.

What Autopilot Really Means

When a plane is put on autopilot, there's still a pilot in the cockpit. The system handles routine adjustments, keeps the plane level, and follows the route. The human remains there to step in if something unusual happens.

This is the ideal for algorithmic decision-making:

- AI manages routine cases
- Humans handle the unusual, the ambiguous, or the moral
- But we have drifted into something different:
- Systems don't just assist, they define choices
- Humans become supervisors in name, but rubber stamps in practice
- Organizations forget what it's like to operate without automation

Autopilot in society is increasingly common. Recommendation systems decide what you see, who you connect with, and even what you get angry about. Credit and risk models determine whether you can rent an apartment or secure a loan. Automated filters narrow down job applicants before a human ever sees their résumé. Predictive policing tools send officers to some neighborhoods and not others. Welfare and insurance algorithms approve or deny claims with very little human review.

None of these systems is fully autonomous in the science-fiction sense. People built them, signed contracts, and wrote the policies. Yet, for most people, the only thing visible is the output: "approved," "denied," "recommended," "flagged." The decision arrives dressed as fact.

The Three Layers of Autopilot

Society on autopilot isn't the flip of a single switch. It is a stack of systems, each nudging something essential.

1. The Attention Layer

Here live the recommender systems:

- Social media feeds pick what you see first
- Video platforms line up your next clip
- News aggregators decide which stories are visible and which are buried
- Search engines autocomplete your queries and rank answers

These platforms are optimized for engagement, not for truth or well-being. They learn what keeps you scrolling and clicking, and then give you more of it. Over time, this shapes your sense of what matters, what's normal, and what is urgent. The system doesn't command you directly; it nudges your attention, over and over, until your reality bends to what performs best in the metrics.

2. The Administrative Layer

This is the world of forms, points, and eligibility:

- Credit scores and fraud scores
- "Risk assessments" used in policing or child protection
- Automated grading in schools
- Screening tools in hiring

Here, AI affects not just what you see but what you can do. The model might rank job candidates before interviews, flag a loan applicant as high-risk, recommend removing a child from a home, or suggest a longer prison sentence. Officials claim these tools are "advisory," but when caseloads are heavy and time is short, advisory outputs often become the default.

3. The Infrastructure Layer

This layer is quieter but crucial:

Traffic systems that adjust lights and tolls

Power grids balancing energy loads

Content moderation removing posts and accounts

Spam filters deciding which emails you see

Most of these work well enough that we barely notice them—until they don't. A moderation glitch removes posts about a protest. A spam filter swallows an important legal notice. A routing algorithm diverts trucks through residential streets. In this layer, autopilot isn't just about individual fairness but about robustness. What happens when a system fails quietly but at scale?

Human in the Loop—On Paper

Nearly every system like this promises reassurance: "A human is always in the loop."

In theory, this means:

▶ The human reviews the model's reasoning

▶ They have time and context to disagree

▶ Their judgment counts

▶ Overrides are tracked and used to improve the system

In practice, the reality looks different. The human often sees only the output—a risk score, a recommendation. They are told to move quickly. Their own performance is measured by how closely they follow the system's advice. Overriding the model feels risky and is rare.

The loop exists, but the direction of influence has flipped. The human is in the machine's loop, not the other way around. This shift shows up everywhere: doctors who must justify when they deviate from AI-generated treatment plans, caseworkers audited for "variance" from risk scores, teachers told that algorithmic grading is more objective than their own assessment.

When your job is measured by how often you disagree with the machine, you quickly stop disagreeing. Autopilot doesn't just supplement; it becomes the norm.

Metrics as a Trap

Autopilot systems are driven by metrics:

- Click-through rates
- Watch time
- Conversion rates
- Default rates
- Risk reduction
- Cost savings

Metrics themselves aren't bad. Without them, there is no way to measure progress. The problem comes when hitting the metric becomes the only goal.

If customer support is rated by "call resolution time," agents will rush calls, even when people need more help. If police are rated by "crime reduction in targeted zones," they might focus on arrest numbers instead of safer communities. If a welfare agency is measured on "fraud reduction," it may design systems that aggressively cut off borderline cases, denying support to many who need it.

AI is a powerful optimization engine. Give it an objective—any objective—and it will search for a way to achieve it. Show more sensational content to drive engagement, over-flag certain groups to reduce defaults, or prioritize easy-to-deny claims to keep payouts low. When objectives are misaligned with human values, AI will faithfully optimize us into harm.

We like to blame the algorithm. More often, the trouble starts with the targets we set.

Feedback Loops That Lock In Inequality

Autopilot systems do not operate in a vacuum. They create feedback loops that reinforce themselves.

Predictive policing is a classic example:

▶ Historical arrest data shows more crime in certain neighborhoods.

▶ The model predicts crime will happen there again.

▶ Police are sent more often to those neighborhoods.

▶ More policing means more recorded crime and more arrests, even if behavior hasn't changed.

▶ The new data confirms the model's original bias.

Similar loops appear elsewhere. If a credit model downgrades people from certain zip codes, fewer loans go to those neighborhoods, leading to economic decline and justifying yet more downgrading. If hiring screens favor graduates from elite schools, those schools gain more prestige and the cycle repeats. If recommender systems amplify polarizing content, public discourse hardens and moderate voices are drowned out.

The system doesn't "know" it's biased. It follows the data and the metric. But if you're on the wrong side of these loops, the effect feels like fate. The same neighborhoods are over-policed, the same groups under-hired, and the same people scrutinized more than others. The danger isn't a single unfair decision; it's inequality solidifying, year after year.

Deskilling Institutions

There's another side effect to life on autopilot: institutions forget how to operate manually.

A generation of workers is growing up on:

▶ Automated templates
▶ Risk scores
▶ "Smart" routing
▶ Dashboards for everything

They learn the tools more than the underlying judgment. Some of that is progress; tools can make us better. But when tools become crutches, problems emerge.

Doctors may trust diagnostic prompts over their own instincts, even when something feels off. Loan officers cannot explain decisions they've never made without a model. Judges defer to sentencing guidelines generated by opaque risk tools instead of fully considering individual circumstances.

When these systems fail, due to outages, cyberattacks, or policy changes, institutions struggle to adapt. If errors creep in, few people remember what "right" looks like without the model. Autopilot boosts efficiency but also increases fragility.

The Comfort of Not Deciding

Autopilot isn't just about savings or speed. It's about comfort.

Saying "the system decided" feels safer than "I decided." Denials and rejections sting less when they come from a web portal instead of a person across a desk. Politicians can blame algorithms for unpopular outcomes, while still taking credit for increased efficiency.

For overworked staff, automated decisions bring relief: fewer files to review, fewer confrontations, and a sense that someone or something else shares the responsibility. The model becomes a shield. When things go wrong, you can say, "We followed procedure."

But there's a cost. People harmed by wrong decisions often can't find anyone who feels responsible enough to fix them. Mistakes that would be obvious face-to-face slip through a stream of numbers. Institutions drift from serving people to merely administering outcomes.

We never set out to replace human judgment with machine outputs. We set out to make life easier, and quietly accepted a trade we never fully examined.

Invisible Governance

When we talk about "government," we picture elections, laws, courts, politicians. But most of the decisions shaping daily life happen far from parliaments or congresses.

They happen in:

Procurement contracts with software vendors

Internal memos about risk thresholds

Technical specifications for IT systems

This is where autopilot is built.

A welfare agency doesn't pass a law saying, "We will deny claims more aggressively to meet budget constraints." It signs a contract for a "decision-support system" that promises "fraud reduction" and "efficiency gains." It tweaks a parameter in a dashboard.

A police department doesn't publicly declare, "We will prioritize surveillance in poorer neighborhoods." It buys a predictive tool trained on past arrest data, call volume, and occupancy rates.

A bank doesn't vote to make lending tougher for young people or immigrants. It upgrades to a new underwriting model that weighs "stability indicators" such as age, property ownership, or length of residence, which correlate with privilege.

These choices aren't always debated in public. They're embedded in technical decisions, made quietly, and then left to run—autopilot, for society.

The rise of autopilot is not just a technical shift. It is a political and social transformation that risks trading accountability, judgment, and fairness for efficiency, comfort, and plausible deniability. If we want to regain control, we need to make these invisible systems visible again and demand that real people, not just algorithms, stand behind the decisions that shape our lives.

CHAPTER 10

Reclaiming Control

If you tune into enough AI talk shows, you start to hear the same question repeated, almost like a drumbeat.

"So... is it too late?"

Is it too late to save jobs?

Too late to protect elections?

Too late to rein in surveillance?

Too late to avoid building something we can't control?

The message underneath is always the same: this technology is happening to us. Someone else built it, someone else profits, and the rest of us are just along for the ride.

This chapter is about refusing that posture.

We don't get to decide whether AI exists. That choice was made for us, many times, by governments, investors, and executives. But we still have choices left:

Where it's allowed.

Under what conditions.

With what rights for the people it affects.

Reclaiming control doesn't mean pretending we can pack the technology up and send it away. It means deciding, together, what we will and won't tolerate—and creating institutions sturdy enough to hold the line.

Step One: Draw Bright Lines

When people talk about AI governance, the conversation often gets vague. We hear things like:

"We should make sure it's used for good."

"We need ethical AI."

"We must balance innovation and safety."

These phrases look great in press releases, but they rarely constrain anyone.

Real control starts with bright lines—clear uses we don't permit, no matter the profit, convenience, or hype.

Every society will draw these lines differently, but some candidates come up again and again in public surveys and debates:

No biometric mass surveillance.

No constant face recognition in public.

No default tracking of everyone's movements and social ties.

No AI as the final authority on life essentials.

No fully automated denial of welfare, healthcare, or asylum without a responsible human decision-maker.

No "computer says no" blocking what people need to survive.

No lethal autonomous weapons without meaningful human control.

No systems that select and kill targets on their own.

No software loopholes to skirt the laws of war.

No non-consensual sexual deepfakes or "nudification" tools.

Treat them as image-based sexual abuse, not "content."

Platforms must be required to remove and trace these quickly.

No hidden scoring of citizens into "good" and "bad" categories.

No secret social credit that shapes access to jobs, housing, or travel.

You don't need a degree in computer science to have opinions on these. They are about values, not technical details.

When bright lines are real, they become more than slogans. They give:

Regulators clear mandates instead of fuzzy goals.

Companies unambiguous "no-go" zones.

Citizens something specific to defend and expand.

Without those lines, everything becomes a gray area. "Ethics" turns into a workshop topic, not a constraint.

Step Two: Put People Back in the Loop

Earlier, we saw how "human in the loop" often becomes a comforting fiction. Reclaiming control means making this a right, not a marketing slogan.

For AI systems that materially affect someone's life—jobs, credit, housing, benefits, education, policing—three rights are non-negotiable.

The right to know when AI is used.

People deserve clear notice when decisions are significantly shaped by automated systems. No secret scoring, profiling, or "experiments" on unwitting populations.

The right to an explanation.

Not just "your application was denied," but which factors mattered, how they were weighed, and what you can change. Explanations must be in plain language, not buried in legal or technical jargon.

The right to contest and to human review.

There must be a clear, accessible way to say, "The system is wrong," and to have a human review the case. That human must have the time and authority to overrule the algorithm without getting punished for "non-compliance."

These rights are only meaningful if backed by deadlines, enforceable penalties, and real support—like ombuds offices, legal aid, or advocacy groups. Without these, "you can appeal" becomes "good luck shouting into the void."

Step Three: Redesign Work Around People

AI doesn't have to be jobless by design. That is a choice, not a law of nature.

The current economic structure pushes companies to cut labor costs, automate aggressively, claim "efficiency," and move on.

Reclaiming control at work means flipping the default. Use AI to make jobs better, not just cheaper.

That requires:

Worker say over deployment.

Unions and worker councils should have formal veto or negotiation rights before new AI systems launch. Mandatory impact assessments must include worker perspectives.

Rules for algorithmic management.

Ban purely automated firing and disciplinary actions. Be transparent about data collection, how it's used, and what performance metrics mean. Limit invasive tracking—no 24/7 surveillance of keystrokes, eye movements, or bathroom breaks.

Sharing the gains.

If AI boosts productivity, some of that value should go to higher wages, shorter hours, or better benefits—not just to executives and shareholders. Experiment with reduced workweeks, backed by real productivity data.

Pathways, not cliffs.

If a role is being automated, employers should provide advance notice, retraining opportunities, and realistic alternative roles—not just a farewell email and a list of online courses.

Individually, workers can't stop automation. But collectively, through unions, professional associations, and political pressure, they can shape how it lands.

If you accept AI's impact on work as "just the market," you have already surrendered. Markets are made of rules and power. Both can change.

Step Four: Make Procurement Democratic

Much of AI enters public life through procurement—contracts between governments and vendors.

Most of these deals are nearly invisible. They are negotiated by small teams, rushed, framed as technical upgrades, and shielded by "trade secrets" and NDAs.

This must flip. AI in public services should be treated as public infrastructure, not a cloud subscription.

Some basics:

Transparency by default.

Governments should keep public registries of the AI systems they use—what they do, who makes them, what data they use, and how they were tested. Plain-language summaries must be available alongside technical documents.

Public input before deployment.

Community hearings or consultations should precede adoption of AI in policing, welfare, education, or healthcare. Independent civil society reviews—beyond vendor slides and internal memos—are essential.

Performance and fairness clauses.

Contracts should require vendors to meet accuracy, bias, and robustness benchmarks, or else face penalties and loss of the contract. Vendors must support external audits and address issues detected by regulators or watchdogs.

Exit ramps.

Clear procedures must allow a system to be switched off if it causes harm, including data portability so agencies aren't trapped with a single vendor.

If a city can hold public meetings about bus lines, it can do the same for predictive policing or welfare algorithms. These systems shape lives just as much.

Step Five: Build Technical Guardrails

Policies and laws are vital, but some guardrails need to be inside the technology itself.

A few shifts matter most:

Safety by design.

Evaluate models for misuse and bias before they go into products, not after a PR crisis. Red-teaming must be a core part of development.

Capability gating.

Don't give general users direct access to high-risk features (like advanced bio, cyber, or surveillance tools). Put dangerous tools behind verification, logging, and oversight.

Privacy-preserving defaults.

Minimize data collection. Strip or disguise identifiers where possible. Use real privacy tools—like differential privacy—only when they actually reduce risk.

Documented limits.

Every model should come with clear, empirically tested accounts of what it can't do reliably. Developers must publish known failure modes, not just cherry-picked successes.

Open evaluation, not necessarily open weights.

You don't have to open-source everything, but there must be meaningful scrutiny—benchmarks, third-party audits, shared red-team reports.

If a company claims a model is safe enough for millions, it should be able to demonstrate that to someone besides its own PR team.

Step Six: Rewrite the Social Contract

AI amplifies a deeper problem: our basic survival is tied to unstable labor markets. If your ability to pay rent or feed your kids depends on holding a job at a particular moment, any technological shock can be a disaster.

Untangling this is political, but essential. Some options:

Stronger unemployment and transition support, especially for workers displaced by automation.

Retraining that leads to real jobs, not just "learn to code" slogans.

Experiments with universal basic income or cash floors, alongside strong public services.

Shorter standard workweeks to share productivity gains.

Tax structures that stop rewarding indiscriminate automation.

If we keep the old social contract—"you're on your own, good luck"— every wave of AI deployment will widen the gap between those who ride the changes and those left behind.

Step Seven: Change Everyday Habits of Trust

Institutions matter, but so do daily habits.

Individual choices won't solve systemic AI harms, but they shape the culture and can blunt some worst effects.

A few practical shifts:

- **Pause before sharing.** Treat dramatic videos and screenshots with skepticism. Check sources and look for corroboration.
- **Set boundaries with AI tools.** Don't feed them more personal data than necessary. Be cautious about generating intimate or sensitive content.

- **Resist anthropomorphism.** Don't act as if systems are friends or therapists. Remember they're pattern machines, not people.
- **Support targets, not just talk.** If someone is hurt by deepfakes, discrimination, or errors, treat it as real harm. Share resources and push institutions to act.
- **Teach critical AI literacy.** In classrooms, families, and workplaces, talk about how these systems work—and fail. Explain that AI can be wrong, biased, or manipulative even when it looks polished.

These habits alone won't fix structural problems. But they help build a norm that doesn't shrug at AI misuse or treat it as inevitable.

Step Eight: Make It Global, or It Won't Work

AI is not a local phenomenon. Models trained in one country can be deployed everywhere. Data extracted from one region can be used to power products sold back to it.

To avoid digital colonialism, a few principles matter:

- **Voice for the Global South.** Countries most affected by AI must have real influence in setting global norms, not just be "consulted" after decisions are made.
- **Technology transfer with dignity.** Rich states shouldn't hoard AI expertise and benefits. Partnerships should build local capacity, not just export finished systems.
- **Avoid dumping grounds.** Stop exporting banned or restricted AI products to countries with weaker protections. Set global standards to prevent treating some populations as test beds.
- **Shared crisis planning.** Build mechanisms for dealing with cross-border AI incidents—deepfake-driven conflicts, cyberattacks, or model failures affecting multiple countries.

If AI is going to shape the next century of development, every region deserves more than a footnote in someone else's framework.

What You Can Do, Wherever You Are

It's easy to read all this and think, "What can I actually do?"

Here are some ways to push for change:

As a worker or professional:

Join or support unions and professional organizations that address AI issues.

Push for transparency on AI tools used in performance evaluation, hiring, or scheduling.

If you work in tech, refuse to build or deploy harmful systems; support colleagues who raise concerns.

As a voter or citizen:

Ask candidates specific questions about AI in policing, welfare, or schools.

Support policies that give regulators real power, not just talking points.

Show up to local hearings on surveillance tech or city contracts.

As a manager or decision-maker:

Don't deploy AI just because it's trendy. Use it where it truly helps people do their jobs better.

Build opt-out and appeal paths into every system.

Treat safety and fairness checks as essential, not optional.

As an educator or parent:

Teach not just how to use AI tools, but when not to.

Encourage healthy skepticism: "Check it" is better than "Believe nothing."

Talk about consent, privacy, and digital reputation, especially in the age of deepfakes and voice cloning.

None of these alone will change the big picture. Together, they create expectations and pressure that help institutions and regulators go further.

Reclaiming Control Is a Process

There won't be a day when someone flips a switch and announces, "We have now reclaimed control over AI."

Control isn't a destination. It is an ongoing process:

Debating and defending values.

Setting and enforcing limits.

Updating rules as technology evolves.

Listening to those who are harmed and changing course.

We'll make mistakes. Some areas will be overregulated, others too loose. New risks will appear, and benefits may surprise us.

But there's a difference between mistakes made inside a framework of responsibility, and mistakes that happen in a vacuum.

Right now, much of AI deployment lives in that vacuum: thin rules, heavy marketing, little accountability. Reclaiming control means filling the space with something better:

Rights you can invoke.

Institutions you can challenge.

Norms companies must actually respect, not just perform.

The alternative is more autopilot, more "oops, we didn't anticipate that," and more decisions made in rooms where the rest of us are not invited.

In the conclusion, we will tie the threads together:

The myths that slowed us down.

The misuses already reshaping society.

The choices still open to us—if we treat AI not as destiny, but as tools built in our image, for better or worse.

The machines are not in charge. Not yet.

The real question is whether we act like we are.

We built this

Strip away the headlines, the hype, and the jargon. At its heart, this book has been about a single, simple idea:

AI is not something happening to us. It is something we are building, and it will continue to mirror what we choose to value, tolerate, and ignore.

We've walked together through different rooms of the same house. We explored the myths—how AI is sold as neutral, benevolent, or destined to become superhuman. We examined the data economy, which treats our lives as raw material. We saw how AI is reshaping work, often by design, to require fewer people. We looked at the quiet war on truth through deepfakes and synthetic media, and at AI's role as a weapon in conflict and repression. We followed the corporate arms race, where technology labs ship faster than anyone can fully understand. We confronted the governance gap that yawns between what AI can do and what our rules can actually handle. We watched as society slides onto autopilot, letting systems steer by default. And finally, we sketched out how we might reclaim control—without pretending we can turn back time.

None of these themes stands alone. They are all different angles on the same question: power.

Who holds it?

Who loses it?

Who gets to decide what the future is for?

The Story We Were Sold

We were promised AI that would be efficient and objective. We were told it would deliver new prosperity, and take care of the boring stuff. Sometimes, it does. But the gaps are clear.

Systems marketed as neutral often embed old prejudices. Tools that "save time" quietly replace jobs or reduce them to their barest parts. Recommendations that "optimize engagement" can poison our public life.

The biggest lie in the myth of the benevolent machine isn't that AI can't help. It's the idea that harm is just an accident.

What we have called "misuse" across these chapters is rarely a glitch. It is a feature of systems built quickly for narrow goals: to cut costs, win contracts, capture markets, or secure an edge in war or politics. If you ask AI to optimize for any of those goals, and neglect to put up guardrails, it will do exactly what you asked—and trample everything you forgot to mention.

The Future Isn't Written in Code

A dangerous idea keeps returning: that technology has its own unstoppable destiny. Once something can be built, the thinking goes, it's only a matter of time before it is.

But that's not how progress works.

We banned lead in gasoline and paint.

We don't allow every drug simply because it can be synthesized.

We have developed rules—imperfect, evolving, real—for planes, food safety, cars, and nuclear plants.

In every case, skeptics warned that we'd kill innovation, that the issues were too complex for lawmakers, or that the market would sort things out. They were wrong often enough that most of us now take those guardrails for granted. We don't call them "anti-technology." We call them civilization.

AI is messier. It's intangible, fast, and entangled with old problems: inequality, weak labor protections, fragile democracies, and unstable information systems. But it is not beyond our reach.

We can still make choices:

Decide where AI simply does not belong.

Demand transparency and appeal rights for high-stakes decisions.

Penalize designs that predictably hurt people.

Restrict access to especially dangerous capabilities.

Invest in public-interest alternatives instead of just corporate platforms.

We can also refuse every argument that starts with "we have no choice."

What "Control" Really Means

Regaining control isn't about micromanaging code. It's about something more grounded:

Owning the consequences. When a system wrongly denies housing or healthcare, there must be a real way to fix it—and a real person who must answer for it. When a platform amplifies abuse or disinformation, "the algorithm did it" isn't a valid excuse.

Aligning incentives with values. Right now, profit, speed, and scale are rewarded; caution, fairness, and responsiveness are paperwork. We can flip those signals—through laws, contracts, pressure, and where we direct our time and money.

Keeping humans meaningfully in charge. We need people who aren't just rubber stamps, but actual decision-makers with power, responsibility, and the right to say no to the machine's suggestions.

Control does not mean nothing ever goes wrong. It means that, when things do go wrong, we don't shrug and point at the machine. We change the machine—or we turn it off.

Fear, Hope, and the Space Between

At this moment in history, it's easy to drift toward one of two emotions.

Fear imagines only catastrophe: jobless cities, untrustworthy media, autonomous weapons, systems spiraling out of control.

Hype imagines only salvation: AI curing every illness, ending scarcity, solving the climate crisis, fixing human flaws.

Reality will be more complicated—and more boring—than either story.

We will almost certainly see impressive breakthroughs alongside embarrassing failures. There will be real cures and real risks, genuine productivity gains and ugly new forms of exploitation. Some tools will help us learn, create, and connect. Others will isolate, mislead, and control.

It's not about whether AI will be good or bad. It will be both. The question is:

Which parts do we amplify, and which do we push back on—hard?

This isn't just a task for developers or regulators. It's for everyone: workers deciding what they'll accept, voters choosing their policies, educators shaping how students learn to think, journalists deciding how to cover AI without fueling hype or doom, and families setting the norms they want in their own circles. You are already part of that answer, whether you wanted to be or not.

The Smallest Level Where It Matters

It's easy to believe that, unless you're writing laws or training models, your choices don't count.

But AI misuse becomes real through small, everyday decisions:

A school district buys proctoring software that treats every student as a potential cheat.

A manager installs keystroke trackers instead of talking to their team.

A newsroom uses AI to churn out low-quality content for ad revenue.

A friend shares a fake video because it matches their beliefs.

Each decision is tiny compared to "the future of AI." Yet together, they are the future of AI—at least the part most people actually experience.

At this level, reclaiming control can look like:

Showing up at a school board meeting.

Pushing back at work against invasive monitoring.

Refusing to chase clicks with garbage content.

Asking, "Where did this come from?" before you hit "share."

None of this alone will stop autonomous weapons or fix the corporate arms race. But this is how norms form. And norms, multiplied, become politics.

The Big Things Still Worth Fighting For

Zoom out again, and some non-negotiables become clear:

A right to a fair shot.

No one's life chances should be defined by unaccountable scores and models.

A right to privacy and dignity.

Our faces, voices, bodies, and movements shouldn't be endlessly harvested, cloned, or traded without real consent.

A right to truthful, plural information.

We may never erase lies, but we can demand platforms and institutions that don't prefer them by design.

A right to meaningful work and rest.

If AI increases productivity, that surplus should go in part to the people whose labor and data make it possible, not just to shareholders.

A right to decide how deadly force is used.

No society should drift into a world where machines choose who lives and dies without transparent, democratic choice.

These are not "AI rights." They are human rights, updated for a new age. AI only makes the consequences of ignoring them faster, bigger, and harder to undo.

One Last Image

Think of AI not as a single looming entity, but as a construction site sprawling across the world.

Everywhere you look, someone is pouring concrete—building the infrastructure, the models, the chips. Others are raising scaffolding—apps, platforms, interfaces. Still others draft blueprints—policies, safety plans, standards.

Some parts of the site are beautiful. Some are obviously dangerous. Others are half-built and already cracking.

You didn't ask for this project. You might not like the architects. But you live in the building, regardless.

Reclaiming control doesn't mean tearing it all down. It means walking the site with your eyes open, marking off unsafe areas, insisting on inspections, and changing the plans when you see they lead somewhere you refuse to live.

Above all, remember: none of this is natural or inevitable.

We built this.

And we can still choose what we're building toward.

A Practical Guide to Living With AI (Without Letting It Run You)

This isn't a whole extra chapter—think of it as a field kit for real life. Use it as needed.

1. For Everyday Life

When you see something online:

- Before you believe or share, pause.

Check the source:

- Is it from a known outlet or person, or a random account?
- Has this source been reliable before?

Look for corroboration:

- Can you find the same event reported by at least two or three independent, credible sources?
- If it's only on one sketchy page or in a single screenshot, treat it as unconfirmed.

Interrogate the content:

- Does the video or audio have odd lip sync, flickering, strange hands, warped text, or weird shadows?
- Is the emotional tone too perfect—clearly designed to make you furious or terrified?

Ask yourself: Who benefits if I believe this?

> ▶ Does it neatly confirm what "my side" wants to think?
>
> ▶ Would someone gain power, clicks, or money if this goes viral?

When in doubt: don't share it. Silence spreads slower than lies.

> ▶ You don't have to debunk everything you see. Simply refusing to pass on what you're not sure about already helps.

When you use AI tools (chatbots, image generators, etc.):

> ▶ Treat them as smart calculators, not oracles.

Use them to:

> ▶ Draft and refine emails, letters, and outlines
>
> ▶ Brainstorm ideas and perspectives
>
> ▶ Summarize long texts (but spot-check the summary)
>
> ▶ Practice languages, rehearse conversations, explore "what ifs"

Don't use them to:

> ▶ Make irreversible legal, medical, or financial decisions without a qualified human
>
> ▶ Draft anything intimate you'd be devastated to see leaked
>
> ▶ Fully outsource your own thinking or writing—especially for things that matter to you

Three short rules:

> ▶ Trust, but verify. Always double-check facts.
>
> ▶ Assume no privacy. Don't put in secrets you can't afford to lose.
>
> ▶ Remember, there is no "it" in there. There's no soul, no therapist, no friend—just a machine predicting the next word.

When someone is hurt by AI (and it's not you):

If a friend, colleague, or family member is hit by:

- A deepfake
- An obviously unfair algorithmic decision (loan, job, benefits)
- Invasive surveillance at work or school
- Your response matters more than you might think.
- Take it seriously. "It's just online" is not helpful.
- Help them document: screenshots, emails, timestamps, links

Encourage them to:

- Appeal formally through the company or agency
- Reach out to a digital-rights group or legal-aid organization

If they want to go public:
Help them share their story safely
Support them if trolls or skeptics pile on

Normalizing solidarity is part of pushing institutions to change.

2. For Workplaces

If you're a worker (at any level):

- When your employer introduces AI, ask specific questions:
- What data about me is collected?
- How is it used to evaluate or manage my work?
- Can I see my profile or score?
- Can I challenge it if it's wrong?

Watch for red flags:

- Secret monitoring: keyloggers, screen scraping, constant webcam use
- Purely automated firing or discipline
- "The system says you're underperforming" with no explanation

Act together where you can:

Talk with coworkers: is everyone seeing the same patterns?

Use unions or form worker groups to negotiate:

- ▶ Limits on tracking
- ▶ The right to human review
- ▶ Consultation before AI deployment

You're not "anti-technology" for wanting guardrails. You're pro-human.

If you're a manager or team lead:

Your choices quietly set the tone.

Before deploying a new AI system:

Define the purpose clearly. "Reduce paperwork" is very different from "monitor everyone more closely."

Pilot small, with consent. Start with volunteers, then ask:

- ▶ Did this make your job easier?
- ▶ What felt creepy, confusing, or unfair?

Guarantee three things:

- ▶ No one will be fired solely by an automated decision
- ▶ People can see and correct the data used about them
- ▶ There's a straightforward process to appeal system outputs

Measure the right things:

Not just "efficiency," but also:

- ▶ Error rates
- ▶ Employee stress and burnout
- ▶ Turnover
- ▶ Customer complaints

If the tool makes people faster but miserable or error-prone, it isn't truly "productive."

Over time, these small choices become your team's culture—and your small corner of society's autopilot.

3. For Schools, Parents, and Students

For educators:

Make AI literacy part of the curriculum: what these systems are and aren't, how to spot AI-generated media, ethics around plagiarism, consent, and privacy

Be honest about use: Are you using AI for grading or feedback? Tell students. Give them a way to contest AI-marked errors.

Resist:

▶ Constant proctoring that treats everyone as a cheat

▶ Tools that hoover up student data for profit

A question to ask of every ed-tech product: Does this help human teaching, or just try to replace it on the cheap?

For parents:

Talk to kids about AI like you would about strangers online, advertising, or peer pressure.

Key points:

▶ "It can sound confident and still be wrong."

▶ "It doesn't love you or hate you. It doesn't feel."

▶ "Some images and videos online can be fake but look real."

Model the behavior. When you get a sketchy video or message, say out loud what you're doing:

"This looks intense. I'm going to check if it's real before I believe it."

You're teaching a habit.

You can also give kids language they can use themselves:

"I'm not sure this is real. I'm going to check before I react."

4. For Civic Life and Politics

You don't need to be a policy expert to nudge politics in better directions.

Questions to ask politicians or parties (even one makes a difference):

▶ Should police, welfare, or immigration officials use black-box AI systems? Under what rules?

▶ What rights should I have if an AI system denies me a loan or benefit?

▶ Do you support bans on biometric mass surveillance?

▶ Will you commit to not using deepfakes or AI-generated disinformation in campaigns?

Even asking forces them to think—and signals that voters care.

What to support, in plain terms:

When you see proposals, look for:

Transparency: I get to know if AI was used, and roughly how

Appeal rights: I can challenge an AI-shaped decision and reach a human

Enforcement: Someone can actually fine or restrain companies, not just "encourage them"

Protection: clear illegal status for things like:

▶ Non-consensual sexual deepfakes

▶ Fully automated denial of essentials

"Encouragement" and "principles" are not enough. Look for verbs like "shall," "must," "is prohibited," "liable," "enforced by."

5. A Short Personal Checklist

When you bump into AI in any context, quickly ask yourself:

- What is this system optimizing for? (Profit? Time? Engagement? Safety? Whose?)
- Who could be harmed if it fails or is biased? (Me? My community? Strangers?)

Can I tell when it's wrong? If not, that's a problem.

Is there a human who can overrule it—in practice, not just in theory?

Do I have a way to say "no" or "this isn't acceptable"? If not, that's a structural issue, not a personal one.

You won't always be able to fix the situation. But you'll be clear-eyed about what you're dealing with—and better able to join others pushing for change.

6. One Last Thing

You don't have to:

Understand every technical detail

Have a perfect take on AGI timelines

Or follow every AI summit

to have legitimate, important opinions about how AI shows up in your life.

You already have the key tools:

A sense of fairness

A sense of dignity

A sense of what feels human and what doesn't

Everything in this book has been an extended argument for this:

You are allowed to use those instincts on technology, too.

Key Terms and Concepts (Plain-Language Glossary)

Use this as a quick reference when thinking about AI and its impact.

Artificial Intelligence (AI)

A broad term for systems that perform tasks we usually associate with human intelligence—like recognizing patterns, generating language, or making recommendations. Most of today's AI is "narrow," meaning it's good at specific tasks, not at general understanding like a person.

Machine Learning (ML)

A way of building AI without hard-coding every rule. Instead, developers feed data into algorithms that learn patterns and relationships, then use those patterns to make predictions or decisions.

Training Data

The information used to teach an AI system.

For language models: text from books, websites, code, and other sources.

For image models: huge collections of images and captions.

Whatever is in the data becomes part of what the model "learns"—including biases and stereotypes.

Model (or AI Model)

The mathematical object that results from training. Think of it as a complex function: you put in inputs (text, images, numbers), and get outputs (answers, classifications, predictions), all based on what it learned from the data.

Large Language Model (LLM)

A type of AI model trained on massive amounts of text to predict the next word (or token) in a sequence. Although their goal is simple, LLMs can answer questions, write essays, generate code, and have conversations. They don't "understand" like humans—they're powerful pattern machines.

Generative AI

AI that creates new content: text, images, audio, video, code. It doesn't just label or detect; it actually produces things.

You meet generative AI when you use chatbots, image generators, auto-writing features, voice-cloning apps, and some "smart" slide or code helpers.

Deepfake

Synthetic audio or video that makes it look or sound like someone did or said something they never did. Often created with deep learning. Deepfakes can be used for satire, but also for fraud, harassment, blackmail, and political manipulation.

Algorithmic Bias

When an AI system treats certain groups unfairly, often because of bias in its training data or the way it was designed. For example:

▶ Hiring tools that downgrade women
▶ Risk scores that label Black defendants as "high risk" more often
▶ Facial recognition that works worse on darker-skinned faces
▶ Bias isn't always intentional, but it's still harmful.

Model "Hallucination"

When an AI confidently outputs something factually wrong or made up, like fake citations, incorrect numbers, or invented quotes. The model isn't lying—it doesn't know the truth. It's just producing text that looks plausible based on its training.

Alignment

Efforts to make AI systems behave in line with human values and intentions. This includes:

- Avoiding obviously harmful behavior (such as helping to build weapons)
- Following user instructions when reasonable
- Not pursuing goals that conflict with safety
- "Misalignment" is when systems behave in ways we don't want or expect.

Frontier Model / Frontier AI

A large, cutting-edge AI model considered among the most capable at a given time. Usually, these models are expensive to train and have broad abilities (like coding, reasoning, or working with text and images). They raise special safety concerns, including risks for biosecurity, cybersecurity, and large-scale manipulation.

General-Purpose AI (GPAI)

AI models that can be used for many different tasks and industries, not just one narrow purpose. For example, a general chatbot API that powers customer service, tutoring, and coding help. Regulators often treat GPAI differently due to its wide range of uses and potential misuses.

Autonomy (in AI systems)

How much a system can act on its own:

- Human in the loop: AI suggests, a human decides.
- Human on the loop: AI acts, a human can monitor and override.
- Human out of the loop: AI acts without real-time human control.

For high-stakes areas (war, welfare, policing), many argue that "human out of the loop" should never be allowed.

Algorithmic Management

Using algorithms to monitor, evaluate, and direct workers: setting targets, assigning tasks, tracking performance, and sometimes even making firing decisions. Common in warehouses, delivery apps, call centers, and increasingly in white-collar jobs.

Surveillance Capitalism

An economic model where companies collect vast amounts of behavioral data about people, turn it into predictions about what they'll do, and sell that data to advertisers, politicians, and others. AI makes prediction and manipulation more targeted.

Data Broker

A company in the business of collecting, combining, and selling people's data (like locations, purchases, interests)—often from sources people didn't know were sharing it. This data is then used for ads, risk scores, and more.

Risk Score / Risk Assessment

A numerical rating generated by an algorithm that estimates how likely something is to happen, such as:
Likelihood of repaying a loan
Likelihood of reoffending
Likelihood of committing fraud
These scores can heavily influence decisions about money, freedom, and opportunity.

Black Box

A system whose inner workings are opaque or too complex to interpret. Many AI models are effectively black boxes: we can test and measure them, but it's hard to explain why they produced a particular output.

Red-Teaming

Deliberately trying to break or exploit a system—pushing it to misbehave, leak secrets, or help with harmful tasks. Good red-teaming finds weaknesses before real attackers do.

Safety-by-Design

Building safety into AI from the very beginning: with testing, constraints, monitoring, and guardrails as part of development, not just as last-minute patches.

Governance

The combination of laws, regulations, norms, contracts, and practices that control how AI is built and used. This includes not just "government," but also company policies, standards groups, and public pressure.

"Human in the Loop" (properly understood)

Not just a checkbox. For it to be real:
Humans know when AI is influencing a decision
They have the time and authority to disagree
They are trained and supported to override the system when needed
Otherwise, it's just human rubber-stamping.
Use this glossary whenever you need a refresher on how AI terms show up in the world around you.

The Myth of the Benevolent Machine

BBC News. "A-levels and GCSEs: How did the grading system go so wrong?" August 2020.

Angwin, Julia, et al. "Machine Bias." *ProPublica*, May 2016.

Dastin, Jeffrey. "Amazon Scraps Secret AI Recruiting Tool That Showed Bias Against Women." *Reuters*, October 2018.

Henley, Jon. "Dutch Government Faces Collapse Over Child Benefits Scandal." *The Guardian*, January 2021.

Data Is the New Oil, and It's Toxic

Humby, Clive. "Data Is the New Oil." 2006.

See also: "The World's Most Valuable Resource Is No Longer Oil, but Data." *The Economist*, May 2017.

Federal Trade Commission. *Data Brokers: A Call for Transparency and Accountability*. May 2014.

Information Commissioner's Office (ICO). "ICO Fines Clearview AI Inc £7.5m for Using Images of People in the UK and Orders Them to Stop Obtaining and Using the Data." May 2022.

Federal Trade Commission. Inquiry into "Surveillance Pricing," launched July 2024.

Jobless by Design

World Economic Forum. *The Future of Jobs Report*. 2023.

McKinsey & Company. *The Economic Potential of Generative AI*. June 2023. (References the estimate that up to 30 percent of hours worked could be automated by 2030.)

Brussels Institute for Geopolitics. "The Amazonian Era: The Gigification of Work." 2023.

Deepfakes, Fake News, and the Death of Truth

Vosoughi, Soroush, et al. "The Spread of True and False News Online." *Science* 359, no. 6380 (2018).

Home Security Heroes / Sensity AI. *State of Deepfakes*. (Estimate: Approximately 98 percent of deepfake videos online are non-consensual pornography.)

AI as a Weapon

United Nations Security Council. Final Report of the Panel of Experts on Libya Established Pursuant to Resolution 1973 (2011). March 2021.

"Google Is Helping the Pentagon Build AI for Drones." Gizmodo, March 2018.

Abraham, Yuval. "'Lavender': The AI Machine Directing Israel's Bombing Spree in Gaza." +972 Magazine / Local Call, April 2024.

United Nations General Assembly. Resolution on Lethal Autonomous Weapons Systems (LAWS), 2024.

The Corporate AI Arms Race

Future of Life Institute. "Pause Giant AI Experiments: An Open Letter." March 2023.

Anthropic. *Responsible Scaling Policy*. 2023; updated 2025.

Google DeepMind. *Frontier Safety Framework*. 2024.

Amazon. *Frontier Model Safety Framework*. 2025.

California State Senate. Bill 53. *Transparency in Frontier Artificial Intelligence Act*, passed 2025.

The Governance Gap

European Union. *Artificial Intelligence Act* (Regulation [EU] 2024/1689). Entered into force August 2024.

Executive Office of the President of the United States. *Executive Order 14110 on the Safe, Secure, and Trustworthy Development and Use of Artificial Intelligence*. October 2023.

The Illusion of Superintelligence

Center for AI Safety. "Statement on AI Risk." 2023.

Future of Life Institute. "Call for a Ban on Superintelligent AI." October 2025.

UK Department for Science, Innovation and Technology. *Frontier AI Capabilities and Risks: Discussion Paper*. 2025.

Brookings Institution. "AI Risks: The Distinction between Existential and Immediate Threats." 2024/2025.

Note: For publication, ensure each entry matches your publisher's preferred citation style. Full bibliographic information (authors, titles, publication details, URLs/DOIs if needed) can be expanded as required.

I am deeply grateful to everyone who provided the structural and emotional support that made this book possible and helped bring its investigation into the misuse of artificial intelligence to light.

To the researchers, labor advocates, and technologists whose insights formed the data-driven foundation of this work, your commitment to transparency in an age of algorithmic opacity is a vital defense against the risks we face.

I want to extend my professional respect to the community of independent authors and international business professionals. Your dedication to excellence has been a constant guide through the noise.

Finally, I hold in my heart those who are no longer here to see this book in print. Your legacy is the quiet force behind every word, and I remain committed to the values of respect and hard work that you instilled in me from the very beginning.

Thank you.

Pafel Dubois writes at the intersection of technology, society, and the everyday human experience. With a degree in International Business and fluency in French, Pafel brings a truly global outlook to his work, exploring how digital systems and corporate structures shape our daily lives.

Born outside the United States and shaped by a tapestry of international perspectives, Pafel thrives on uncovering cultural nuance. His journey as a writer began with a simple fascination: How do people worldwide adapt to, resist, and reshape the systems that surround them? For Pafel, every book is an opportunity to bridge divides, challenge assumptions, and find the human pulse beneath the algorithms.

Whether he's examining the promises and pitfalls of artificial intelligence or crafting upmarket fiction, Pafel's work is driven by a search for meaning and connection in an age of rapid change. Through his writing, he invites readers to look past surface-level trends and rediscover what unites us all.

Connect with Pafel and stay updated on new releases at: www.pafeldubois.com.